Kilkerran Graveyard Revisited
A Second Historical and Genealogical Tour

Previously…

Kilkerran Graveyard Revisited forms a sequel to *An Historical and Geneaological Tour of Kilkerran Graveyard* by the same author and illustrator, published by Kintyre Civic Society in 2006. Copies of the first volume are still available from the Secretary at the address on the back of the title-page of the current volume.

KILKERRAN GRAVEYARD Revisited

by

Angus Martin

With
Illustrations by
George John Stewart

Published by:

The Grimsay Press
An imprint of Zeticula
57, St Vincent Crescent
Glasgow
G3 8NQ
Scotland
http://www.thegrimsaypress.co.uk

and

Kintyre Civic Society (Scottish Charity Number: SC020956)
and available from The Secretary at:
"Dunara",
Lochpark,
Carradale East,
Campbeltown,
Argyll,
PA28 6SG,
Scotland.

The Grimsay Press ISBN 978-1-84530-096-8
Kintyre Civic Society ISBN 978-0-9545845-2-8

Contents

Introduction

On the evening before *An Historical and Genealogical Tour of Kilkerran Graveyard* was launched at Campbeltown Library, on 28 September 2006, I began this sequel. The approach this time is essentially the same, except that most entries are of ampler proportions. While writing the first book, I was by no means certain that there would be another, therefore my inclination was to compress the content. This time my feeling has been that a more expansive treatment was required, and I hope that readers will accept this product as readily as they accepted the first.

I have included, in this compilation, three members of my own family – a great uncle, Neil Martin, a great aunt, Isabella McBride and my maternal grandmother, Barbara Boyle – not least because kinship enables me to offer more penetrating insights into their lives. Some of the potted biographies I offer in this book, and in the earlier one, have of necessity been sanitised. There is much more that could have been included, but which I preferred not to mention in order to avoid offending descendants.

I extend my thanks, for assistance, to John Mactaggart, Campbeltown; Bill McKersie, Pinner; George McSporran, Campbeltown; Ian Davies, Altrincham; the staff of Campbeltown Library, for sourcing materials; my wife Judy for computer and internet work on my behalf; to Kate Singleton of the Kintyre Civic Society for her encouragement, and to all others credited in the References.

Angus Martin
13 Saddell Street, Campbeltown
Argyll PA28 6DN, Scotland

THE GRAVES

Division 1

1. **BLACK.** It is rather hard to credit now, but ice sports were hugely popular in nineteenth century Campbeltown. With the twentieth century, however, came generally milder winters, and these sports naturally declined and disappeared. Curling was played on Durry Loch, Black Loch (behind Ben Gullion) and Auchalochy, and in 1892 a pond was created at Homeston Farm for Campbeltown Curling Club.[1] Ice-skating, too, was popular, particularly on Auchalochy – the reservoir in the hills north of Campbeltown – which offered 'a wide field of ice to skim over'. Local images of skating and curling feature in the extensive collection of photographs taken by the Campbeltown brothers Dennis and Charles MacGrory between 1890 and 1910.[2]

Robert Black

During the first week of December 1875, hard frost set in and the local lochs and reservoirs soon had a good covering of ice, attracting numerous skaters and curlers. Some parts of Auchalochy, however, were of such depth that ice was slow in forming, and these dangerous spots had to be avoided. On Tuesday, 7 December, some lads, who had been at work during the day, decided to enjoy an hour's skating by moonlight. One of them, 15-year-old Robert Black, approached too close to one of the unfrozen patches, and 'before he could recover himself ... was observed plunging about in the water'. A 'scene of intense excitement' ensued. Scarves were tied together to form a line, which was thrown to him, but without effect. Roderick Watson then jumped into the freezing water and tried to rescue Black, but that effort also failed, and Watson himself had great difficulty regaining the ice. 'All this time Black himself was clutching at the ice and trying his best to keep above water but the edge of the ice being so thin it yielded under him every time he tried to get on to it.' After Black had finally disappeared, all the skaters 'sorrowfully left the sad scene and reported the disaster to the authorities'. On the following day a boat was taken to the reservoir and the body recovered.[3]

The boy's mother, Agnes Sharp, who lived at Old Quay Head, was no stranger to tragedy. Her first husband, James Black, was master of the local schooner *Cyclops* – owned by Messrs McKersie & Co., distillers – which foundered off the mouth of Campbeltown Loch on 1 December, 1866, drowning not only him but Agnes's brother Peter Sharp.[4] James and Agnes – also 'Ann' and 'Nancy' in the records – were married on 18/10/1859, and their two other sons died in infancy. James was born in Ballycastle, County Antrim, about 1837, but his parents, Archibald Black and Jane McKinlay, were both from Rathlin Island. Five weeks after James's death, Archibald applied to the Parochial Board in Campbeltown for aid for himself and his wife, 'in consequence of his son, who was his principal support, having been lately drowned and their receiving no assistance from the other sons'. The committee awarded him 3s a week.[5] These Black fishing families – examined in my *Kintyre: The Hidden Past*

2

– are distinct from the family of bakers in Campbeltown, which was founded by Paisley-born Joseph Black (died on 31/5/1880, aged 49) and Mary Currie, and from the Blacks who farmed in Killean and Kilchenzie Parish from the eighteenth century.

Such winter fatalities were fortunately rare, but there is record of at least one other, in January 1908, when William McLean, a 17-year-old fisherman, drowned by falling through ice in the small reservoir below Crosshill.[6]

Division 2

2. **CUNNINGHAM**. A marble Celtic cross, flanked by yew trees, against the northern wall. The name Cunningham originates from a place near Kilmarnock, Ayrshire, first recorded in 1153 as *Cunegan*, a British name of uncertain meaning, though the surname can also represent Irish O *Cuinneagain*.[7] The birthplace of Dr John Cunningham, who is buried here, was Girvan, Ayrshire. He graduated from Glasgow University and afterwards qualified for the Diploma of Public Health from Cambridge University. Campbeltown was his first practice; he arrived in 1871 and remained until his death on 22/12/1918, at the age of 74.

His civic services were many and various. This, of course, was at a time when bureaucrats were thin on the ground, social workers non-existent, and the landed and professional classes were expected to do their bit for the good of the community. Education was his special interest, and to his 'forward policy' as chairman of the Burgh School Board was credited the enhanced status of Campbeltown Grammar, from which, by 1918, pupils could pass directly to university. He was a Justice of the Peace for Argyll and an 'honoured official' of Campbeltown Conservative Club. As part of his extensive medical practice in town and country, he held the post of 'colliery doctor', and earned the respect of the mining families of Drumlemble and Pans; indeed, one of the floral tributes laid on his grave was from 'the women of Drumlemble'.

Sir Charles Cunningham

During the five years prior to his death, Dr Cunningham's health was poor, but he continued his medical practice until two months before the end, when 'a critical illness' compelled him to retire. He was survived by his wife, Isabella Patrick, five sons, and three daughters.[8] The couple met while they were both teaching in Glasgow, and had 13 children between 1874 and 1894.[9] Their youngest son, Second-Lieut Stewart Gordon Cunningham, of the Royal Field Artillery, was killed on 22/10/1917, when a German shell exploded at his battery position. Though commemorated on this stone, he is buried near Ypres.[10]

Another son of Dr Cunningham's, Charles, married Grace Macnish (no. 23). He was awarded the Star of India and, in 1933, a knighthood. Educated at Campbeltown Grammar School, he joined the Indian police in 1904, retiring in 1938 as Inspector General. Fluent in 'the many and varied Indian vernaculars', during the Civil Disobedience of 1929 he 'displayed outstanding ability in tackling huge crowds with the result that there was

4

little bloodshed'[11], and was thereby brought into contact with the great independence leader, Mahatma Gandhi (1869-1948).[12]

Still another son, John 'Jack' Cunningham CIE, MA, LLD (1876-1942), had a distinguished career in India, in education. Upon his retiral in 1931, Dr Cunningham returned to Campbeltown and lived at Askomil End with his unmarried sister Margaret ('Madge') until the house was destroyed by a sea-mine's exploding on the front lawn during the second German raid on Campbeltown, on 9/2/1941. He was a dedicated and industrious member of the Kintyre Antiquarian Society, producing a history of Dunaverty Castle and a survey of the prehistoric forts of Kintyre.[13]

The memory of Madge is honoured among local botanists for her authorship, with A G Kenneth, of the seminal *Flora of Kintyre*, published in 1979, the year of her death. Madge, who was also a keen ornithologist, was born in Campbeltown in 1887 and died at Seabank, Low Askomil. She graduated MA from the University of St. Andrews in 1910 and was a teacher in England for seven years before returning to Campbeltown to care for her parents.[14]

Robert Cuninghame – same name, variant spelling – who farmed Kilkivan, Machrihanish, was a contemporary of Dr Cunningham's. He too was Ayrshire-born, Stewarton in his case. Another contemporary, Major R Y Cunningham, was Rector of Campbeltown Grammar School. Among the initial 12 tacksmen (leaseholders) in the mid-seventeenth century Lowland settlement of Kintyre were two Cunninghams, Cuthbert and James.[15]

3. **HAMILTON/BLACKWOOD.** Two Hamiltons, James of Aitkenhead and James of Ardoch, were among the first batch of Lowlanders who received tacks of land in Kintyre in 1650.[16] In the nineteenth century, bearers of the name were a mixture of Lowland and Irish migrants. In the Census of 1861, 51-year-old Andrew Hamilton and family were recorded in Killeonan Farm, and 68-year-old William Hamilton and family in Christlach. Both belonged to Lanarkshire: Carluke and Lesmahagow respectively. Among the Irish, a County Antrim-born family

Rev. Bruce Blackwood.

established the business of Archibald Hamilton & Son, with a pawn-broker's shop in Bolgam Street and a shop in Main Street for the retail of earthenware and the purchase of scrap metal and rags, etc. In the twentieth century, the most prominent family of the name stemmed from Robert 'Bobbins' Hamilton – fencer, drainer and general handyman – and Euphemia 'Phemie' McIntyre, who reared a family of 12 at East Trodigal Cottage.[17]

Andrew Hamilton, buried here, was born in Ayr. He was for 42 years Town Chamberlain of Campbeltown, retiring in 1921. He died on 23/1/1925 at the age of 75, having been predeceased in 1923 by his wife, Christina Wallace, a daughter of Hugh Wallace, builder in Campbeltown. Two of their sons, Hugh and Willie, commemorated here, were killed in France in the First World War.[18]

A daughter, Annie Nisbet Hamilton, who died on 14/11/1976 at the age of 89, married the Rev Bruce Beveridge Blackwood, BD LRAM (Licentiate of the Royal Academy of Music,) who was minister of Lochend UF Church for more than 50 years. A native of Loch Lomondside, he was educated at Vale of Leven Academy and Glasgow University. He came to Campbeltown in 1910 as assistant to the Rev John McQueen (no. 22), upon whose retiral in the following year he was inducted as minister. A notable footballer, and 'a very fine type of the muscular Christian',[19] he was, along with the Rev C Victor A MacEchern, Castlehill Church, a member of the first Campbeltown Grammar School Former Pupils team, formed in 1919. He earlier played for the famous Queens Park AFC and was capped for Scotland both as an Amateur and a Junior.[20] An excellent pianist and a fine tenor, he could, by general consensus, have had a career in music had he so chosen. He died on 21/4/1968 at the age of 82.

Division 1

4. ARBUCKLE. This headstone of grey marble intrigued me for years. First, the name isn't a local one, though it is essentially Scottish, and I couldn't remember having come across a family of that name in Campbeltown. Second, that puzzling aviation

7

accident – '... the crashing of the Imperial Airways' liner "Vellox" on 10th August 1936 ...' – to which the inscription refers. I didn't, however, have far to look. The story is indeed a local one and was carried in the *Campbeltown Courier*, which reported that the 'freight liner', bound for Paris from Croydon on an 'experimental night trip', crashed at Wallington, Surrey, first striking two houses before landing in a garden and bursting into flames. 'The glare from the blaze lit up the whole of the street. The pavements were littered with broken tiles, and engine parts and other pieces of wreckage were all around.' All four crewmen were killed.[21] Imperial Airways had purchased the bi-plane – built by Vickers in 1931 and registered G-ABKY – in May, 1936. She had just been re-engined with Pegasus III motors, and it was believed that the starboard one failed, owing to fuel supply problems, at 500 ft.[22]

Robert Arbuckle

Robert Arbuckle was one of two wireless operators on the flight. He was 22 years old and the eldest son of John Arbuckle, Dell Road, Campbeltown. After leaving Campbeltown Grammar School, Robert attended Skerry's College, Glasgow, to study for the Civil Service. Engineering and radio, however, were his real interests, so he switched to a course at the Caledonian Wireless College, Glasgow, and qualified after 18 months there. Following a two-year spell as a wireless operator on North Sea trawlers, and just four months before his death, he joined Imperial Airways and was soon to be posted to Cairo.[23]

His body was returned to Campbeltown for burial, and hundreds of townsfolk lined the streets as the cortege passed.[24] There are no other burials recorded on the stone, on the base of which appear the following rhyming couplets from 'The Village', by the English poet George Crabbe (1754-1832).

> 'When honour lov'd and gave thee every charm,
> Fire to thy eye and vigour to thy arm;
> Then from our lofty hopes and longing eyes,
> Fate and thy virtues call'd thee to the skies.'

Robert Arbuckle's mother was Janet McKay Martin, a daughter of Captain Duncan Martin of Dalintober (no. 31). In 2005 I had been in contact on family history matters with a John Arbuckle, Ontario, without having realised his connection with Robert; so, I contacted him again and discovered that he was Robert's younger brother, and had taken a cord at the graveside. The Arbuckle family, he said, were so devastated by Robert's death that they moved to Glasgow to 'start afresh'. The origins of John Arbuckle Snr. are hazy. He spoke with an English accent and appears to have grown up in London.[25]

John Jnr. graduated in 1951 from Glasgow University with honours in French and German, qualified as a teacher, and in 1953 emigrated to Canada, where, in 1961, he took a master's degree in Linguistics, having earlier that summer married Francoise Michot. Both taught for a time in the US, but returned to Canada. His brother Ronnie attended Keil School, graduated with a BSc (Agriculture), and spent the greater part of the Second World War camouflaging RAF airports. He then worked in civil government during the post-war military occupation of Germany, and thereafter in Iraq, Sudan, Chile, and in other foreign postings. From 1965 to 1974 he was employed by the United Nations Food and Agricultural Organization, retiring to Gairloch, then moving to Portugal, where in 1995 he died and is buried.[26]

5. **MACQUARIE**. The inscription on this marble monument, topped by a squat urn, does not explain what Charles Macquarie was doing in Campbeltown when he died on 6/1/1869, only that he was 'son of the late Lieut. Colonel Macquarie of Ulva, Mull'. In fact, he was quartermaster of the Argyll and Bute Artillery Militia* and was buried with military honours three days after his death. On the day of the funeral, the Artillery Militia and Volunteers drew up in front of his house on Longrow. Then the procession set off for Kilkerran, watched along its route by large crowds. The cortege was headed by the Militia and a section of the Rifle Volunteers' brass band, playing 'The Dead March in Saul', followed by reversed arms and muffled drum. At Kilkerran, three volleys of blank cartridge were fired over the grave by the Artillery Militia staff and 33 Volunteers. Macquarie, it was remarked, was 'a great favourite amongst the Militia officers and men'.[27]

Charles Macquarie was a nephew of Major-General Sir Lachlan Macquarie (1762-1824), famously Governor of Australia from 1809 – when he replaced Captain William Bligh of *Bounty* notoriety – until 1821, earning the enduring accolade, 'Father of Australia', and a string of places named in his honour. Lieut-Col Charles (1771-1835), like his brother Lachlan, was born on the island of Ulva, off the west coast of Mull. He married Marianne Willison (c1792-1828), a daughter of the Scottish portrait painter, George Willison. They had five children, of whom Charles, buried here, was the eldest.

Charles was educated by tutors in the main residence of Duart Estate, which his father sold in 1825 to purchase the estate of Ulva, ancestral home of the Macquaries. In 1828, however,

10

Charles's mother Marianne died and 'the family's life in Ulva was a melancholy one'. Charles Snr. died in 1835, but he was seriously in debt, owing to his 'soft-hearted' stewardship in the face of economic reverses, and young Charles, far from inheriting Ulva House and the estates of Ulva and Glenforsa, settled for an apprenticeship in carpentry. He married Margaret Campbell – born in Islay, c 1817, daughter of Dugald Campbell, landed proprietor, and Isabella Hunter – and emigrated to Australia, where the first three of their 10 children were born. Around 1846 they returned to Scotland, living first in Moidart and then in Mull. Following a protracted and ultimately unsuccessful legal action, contesting the will of his dissolute and debt-ridden cousin, Lachlan Macquarie Jnr., Charles turned from farming and joined the Argyll and Bute Militia, in which service he died of bronchitis and pneumonia. His widow died at Strathbungo, Lanarkshire, on 9/3/1879 at the age of 60.[28]

The history of the Ulva Macquaries can be sourced in Jo Currie's *Mull: The Island and its People* (Edinburgh, 2000). Macquarie, or MacQuarrie, as it is usually spelt, represents Gaelic *Mac Guaire*, 'Son of Guaire'.[29]

* The Argyll and Bute Artillery Militia – distinct from the Argyll and Bute Artillery Volunteers – date back to 1798 as the Argyll Militia. Originally an ordinary infantry, in 1859 they became a rifle regiment, and in 1861 a regiment of artillery, the Argyll and Bute Militia Artillery, initially with headquarters at Oban, but moving to Campbeltown in 1863.[30]

6. **BROWN.** At times one would think that people with plain surnames, no matter how interesting and accomplished they might be, are forgotten more quickly than those with unusual names. Should that theory hold, then the case of Dr James Pearson Brown, DSO, TD, MA, MB, FRFPS (Glasgow), JP, might be cited as proof. His was a productive and eventful life, though he spent the greater part of it as a medical practitioner in his native town. For a start, he served through two historic conflicts.

In the Boer War he held the rank of Surgeon Lieutenant in the 5th Volunteer Detachment of the Argyll and Sutherland Highlanders

The Late Dr. James Pearson Brown

Death of Campbeltown's Senior Medical Practitioner

Served Through Two Wars

BY the death of Dr. James Pearson Brown, D.S.O., T.D., M.A., M.B., F.R.F.P.S. (Glasgow), J.P., Campbeltown has lost one of its best known and most highly esteemed citizens. Dr. Brown, who was in his 74th year, passed away in a Glasgow Nursing Home on Saturday, 21st February, after an illness of com-paratively short duration.

Dr James Pearson Brown

and Danc

£30 10s Raised for Cot
at Annual Functi

Following its annual cus
District held its Whist Dri
last Wednesday, in aid of th
Campbeltown and District
pital. Notwithstanding the
entertainments in Southend
War Charities, the Territo
packed—convincing evidence
of Southend people to suppo
tion that is rendering such
vice to the whole community

Captain Taylor, on behal
mittee, thanked the compa
continued support. Appr
ence was made by him to
Dr. J. P. Brown, who had
associated with the Cottage
its inception, and who was s
and so highly respected the
whole of Southend.

While the exact amount
evening had not been ascert
assured by the Committee th
be handed over would excee
previous year.

The prizes were present
Dewar—a former Matron o
Hospital. The winners we
Ladies—1, Mrs J. Fergus
Mitchell; 3, Miss Jean C. Sh
Gentlemen—1, Mr Neil
Peter Galbraith; 3, Mr John

After a vote of thanks had
to Miss Dewar, the Secretar
pital expressed the keen a
the Hospital Managers for
and generous support receive
end District. Their work
when the services of nursin
were being so efficiently a
rendered to the sick members
ing Forces as well as to the
the community, was much
He warmly thanked the Com
who had helped towards the
evening's entertainment.

N.B.—We learn that the a
handed over to the Hospital

Continued from Previous

examining and testing Vo
Detachments. His work wa
so conscientiously that it
Argyll's V.A.D. developing in
force whose worth in peace
war-time has been amply
on numerous occasions.

Dr. Brown was Visiting M
of Witchburn House Hospita
Calton Hospital for many ye
recently appointed Medica
Campbeltown Emergency Hos

He was also an enthusiasti
being a member of St. John's
was a generous giver to
Benevolent Fund. Fitting
his passing was made by
Shepherd, R.W.M., at a mee
Lodge on Friday evening
brethren observed a minute
honour of his memory.

In the realm of sport, his
lay in the Bowling Green an
the town enjoyed a game of
than he did. On three differe
he was elected President o
Bowling Club and his valua

12

and received the Queen's Medal, with four clasps. When the Volunteer Detachment became the 8th Argyll and Sutherland Highlanders, Lieut Brown remained with the local Company and was one of its most popular officers. He was mobilised, with the rank of Major, in August 1914, and ultimately had charge of an ambulance train. In November 1917, at Buckingham Palace, he was presented with the Distinguished Service Order by King George V for his bravery in remaining for three hours with a mortally wounded soldier, Sergeant Dan Thomson of Inveraray, during 'a terrific bombardment from the enemy'.

He was the younger brother of Captain Charles 'Charlie' Mactaggart's mother, Susannah Elizabeth Brown (1869-1935), and his letters from the Front are preserved in the Mactaggart family. An extract from one of those letters, written to his mother on 28/5/1915, expresses the sensitivity and honesty of the man. The final line should be scorched into every warmongering politician's brain. 'Last night was a quiet one fortunately ... Tonight we are going into the trenches for a 3 night spell. I hope we will not have many casualties ... At present the country is beautiful with all sorts of flowers coming into blossom, and where we are now some of the small farmers are staying on working their farms and taking the risk of a shell. They say that if they go away they will lose everything. Of course some of them get killed. I wonder if the people at home will ever realise what war is.'

The remainder of his life – he died at the age of 73 on 21/2/1942 – was devoted to his medical practice and to public service: president of the local branch of the RNLI, county controller of the British Red Cross Society, Justice of the Peace for Argyll, and much else in the way of voluntary commitments. It was, however, as doctor and confidant that his death was most deeply regretted. He certainly did not enrich himself in his practice: 'If he thought that payment for his services would result in any hardship being imposed on a family, he conveniently forgot to render an account, and would decline payment, if offered.'

Dr Brown was educated at George Watson's College, Edinburgh, whence he went to Glasgow University, first graduating as MA and then taking his degrees in medicine. After a period as house surgeon at Paisley Infirmary and as a ships' surgeon, 'seeing much of the world', he returned to Campbeltown and commenced his practice there. He was a son of Thomas Brown, businessman in Campbeltown, and Agnes Pearson, in whose lair he is buried (he never married).[31] Thomas Brown belonged to Ayrshire and came to Campbeltown as a young man. His first business venture was the importation of coal, and he later purchased the local net-making factory.[32] Dr Brown's unmarried sister Nellie was a well-known local personality. The adjacent stone – raised for James Pearson, Supervisor of Inland Revenue, who died on 2/1/1870 – commemorates his mother's family.

The name Brown was widespread in Kintyre from the seventeenth century, with a concentration of Mc ilduins – *Gaelic Mac 'Ille Dhuinn*, 'Son of the Brown Lad' – in the Carradale district, eg Gilchreist in Achinreich, and John, Ivar, and Duncan in Achinsawll, in 1685.[33] Present-day Browns in Campbeltown have a wide range of origins, including Ireland and the Hebrides.

7. **McKERSIE**. This unusual name is absent from GF Black's *The Surnames of Scotland*, and from my own genealogical files prior to the nineteenth century. According to family records, the Kintyre McKersies came from Greenock as builders of roads and bridges – in *Pigot's Directory* of 1837, John McKersie is listed as a builder and stonemason in Church Street, Campbeltown – but the name is now inextricably linked to the history of the whisky industry. The name appears to be peculiar to Ayrshire and represents Gaelic *Mac Fhearghuis*, 'Son of Fergus'.[34]

This McKersie stone – flanked by Mitchell monuments – commemorates the first of the distillers, William (died 2/12/1878, aged 72) and his wife Jane Mitchell (died 30/5/1880, aged 71). She belonged to another prominent distilling family, whose business, Springbank, was the only one to survive the local industry's collapse between the wars (Scotia later resumed production).

Two of William McKersie's sons, John and William, themselves became distillers. They were joint proprietors of Albyn and

Lochruan distilleries and famously rivals in ostentation. William had Craigard villa designed in 1882, which prompted his brother John to instruct the architect, HE Clifford, to build a bigger and grander house, Auchinlee, for him.

William McKersie's wife was Marion McCall of Ayr and they had five children. It was a matter of pride to his eldest son, also William, that in 1883 he was the first baby born in Craigard, for the house was sold in 1940 and became the maternity hospital for Campbeltown and district!

Craigard is now an hotel, in which the builder's great-grandson, Andrew McKersie, and his young son, Robert, stayed in 2004. The second son of William and Marion, Jack, emigrated to Southern Rhodesia before the First World War and, with his four sons, founded a farming dynasty, which is now largely dispersed.

William's brother John, of Auchinlee, married Helen Mitchell and had three children. He was elected to Campbeltown Town Council in 1875, and in 1890 became Provost for two consecutive three-year terms, being succeeded by his brother-in-law, Hugh Mitchell. He died on 7/11/1904 at the age of 64. His son Archibald, a Captain in the Highland Light Infantry, was a fatality of the Dardanelles campaign of 1915. He died on 17 July on the hospital ship *Asturias*, from wounds received five days earlier, and is buried in Alexandria, Egypt.[35]

Although no McKersies remain in Kintyre – the family is dispersed throughout the world – for as long as Campbeltown whisky is made and its history studied, the name McKersie will not be forgotten.

8. **BRODIE.** In the hollow, a monument erected to Martha McArthur and her husband, the Rev Neil Brodie. He was born in 1813, the eldest son of Neil Brolachan, enigmatically described as 'artificer, Campbeltown',[36] and Janet Gilchrist.[37] His early education was in the burgh school, Campbeltown, where one of his schoolfellows was the Rev Dr Norman Macleod (1812-72)*, Chaplain to Queen Victoria and author of *Reminiscences of a Highland Parish* (1867), who 'as a preacher and as a contributor to the religious press ... had few rivals'.[38]

Neil attended the University of Glasgow and was ordained a minister of the Church of Scotland at Kilmarnock in 1842. In the following year, conflict within the established church over the issue of patronage – the right, enshrined in the Patronage Act of 1712, of local lairds to appoint parish ministers regardless of the wishes of congregations – resulted in the dramatic walk-out of some 190 clergy from the General Assembly of 18 May in Edinburgh. Ultimately, a third of the ministers – 474 out of 1203 – broke away and formed the Free Church.[39] Neil Brodie was one of those ministers who 'came out', while Norman Macleod remained within the Established Church. In 1844, Neil became minister of Shandon Free Church, on Gareloch, and remained there until 1862. From 1863 until 1892, the year of his death in Rothesay, he was minister of Pollokshaws West Free Church, though, as the headstone inscription implies by 'Minister Emeritus', he had actually retired and the position latterly was an honorary one. In 1842, he married Martha McArthur, daughter of Alan McArthur, HM Customs, Glasgow.[40] She died on 10/5/1879, and, according to one of his obituaries, he remarried, but had no children by either marriage.[41] He died on 10/3/1892.

In 1861 it was remarked of Neil that he was 'highly regarded for his amiable disposition and popular talents as a preacher'[42]; such qualities, however, are ephemeral, and Neil's sole surviving distinction, the mutant name aside, is his putative authorship of the poem 'Flory Loynachan'. I have already, in *Kintyre: The Hidden Past*[43], referred to this attribution, but only in the briefest of terms. See Appendix 2 for a fuller examination of the poem, its authorship and Flory Loynachan herself.

The surname Brodie, as such, is of territorial origin, from the barony of the name in Moray;[44] but in Kintyre it has no such connection. It actually represents one of the multitude of Gaelic surnames which, for a variety of reasons, were replaced by English or Scottish names, largely in the nineteenth century, but commencing earlier. The story of how Neil – erroneously referred to as 'John' – Brolachan became Neil Brodie is worth quoting:

In his first year at Glasgow University he enrolled in the Latin class. When Professor Ramsay was marking the roll, he came to the name John Brollachan. He stopped, looked up at him and said: 'Where did you get that barbarous name?'

The students laughed.

On the class being dismissed, John, feeling a little mortified, proceeded to the Professor's room and told him that after this he wished to be known as John Brodie.[45]

It would be surprising if Neil Brolachan had changed his name quite so impetuously. Indeed, the entire story seemed suspect to me. Nonetheless, I was intrigued and in 1983 wrote to Michael S Moss, Archivist at Glasgow University, and asked him to search his records. He found that Neil had matriculated as 'Niel Brolachan' in 1830, but that by the time his name appeared in the junior Hebrew class of 1834/5, he had become 'Niel Brodie'. He also observed that William Ramsay was Professor of Humanity from 1831 to 1863.[46] There are clearly discrepancies in the story, but the archival evidence does suggest a basis in truth.

I have also examined the name O'Brolachan/Brolachan – from Gaelic *O Brolchain* – in all its variant spellings in my *Kintyre: The Hidden Past*,[47] to which I refer any reader who may wish to engage with the complexities. The pattern of change, however, became distorted by the settlement in Campbeltown, around 1840, of an Irish family which used the surname Broadley, and variants including Bradley, before adopting Brodie as the standard. As early as 1866, the head of this family is referred to in a newspaper report as 'John Brodie or Bradley'[48] That family – which stemmed from John Broadley of Rathlin and Ballymena-born Margaret Kiargan or McKerral – became prominent in the Campbeltown fishing community, and most – perhaps all – of the local Brodies are so descended.[49] The derivation of the Irish surname Bradley, of which Broadley was a Kintyre variant, is almost certainly also *O Brolchain*.[50]

Kintyre's pre-eminent painter, William McTaggart (1835-1910), had a double Brolochan connection. His mother was Barbara

Brolochan, and his first wife, whom he married in 1863, was Mary Brolochan Holmes. William and Mary were descended from two brothers, Duncan and Neil O'Brolochan, who migrated from Ulster to Barr in Kintyre in the first decade of the eighteenth century. William was descended from Duncan, and Mary from Neil, and they were fourth cousins once removed. As Marjorie Heggen, genealogist of the Holmes family, points out, Sir James Caw, in his 1917 biography of William McTaggart, does not mention that William and Mary were related, only that they had known each other as children in Campbeltown and met again in New Orleans Glen in the summer of 1860.[51]

*Born in Campbeltown during the ministry of his father, also Rev. Norman Macleod (1783-1862), but popularly known as *Caraid nan Gaedheal*, 'Friend of the Gael', and an influential Gaelic writer.

9. **VIGROW**. This is certainly one of the most unusual surnames in Kilkerran, because there appears to have been only one family of the name in Scotland and its origin is unknown, though likely to be 'foreign'. Alexander Vigrow, who died on 5/11/1870 at the age of 58, is described on the gravestone – of a soft sandstone, which is eroding towards illegibility – as 'late of the 42nd Royal Highlanders'. He was born near Perth and enlisted at Edinburgh on 7/8/1828 at the age of 16, when described as 5ft. 4 ins. tall, with fresh complexion, blue eyes and brown hair. He rose through the ranks from drummer to Quartermaster Sergeant, and the greater part of his career was spent abroad: three years in Gibraltar, seven in Malta, almost four in Corfu and four in Bermuda. When discharged in 1852, 'for the purpose of serving on the Militia Staff', he had served 22 years and 83 days. His parents were Joseph Vigrow, mariner, and Anne Fisher, beyond which the family has not yet been traced. Alexander married Amelia Innes, a farmer's daughter from Banff. He came to Argyll as Quartermaster and Paymaster of the Argyll and Bute Militia, 42nd Regiment of Foot, and in the Census of 1861 he and his family were in the Militia barracks at Oban. Between

1861 and 1870, the family moved to Campbeltown, where one of the daughters, Emma Vigrow, married William Cuthbertson, farmer in Low Ballywilline, on 6/2/1882. Emma died during childbirth on 26/5/1894 at the age of 35, leaving a son, William, and daughter, Emma. Though the name Vigrow has vanished from Kintyre like many other, and far more common, names, the Vigrow genes persist. One example will suffice: William Cuthbertson Jnr. married Margaret Smith of Bleachfield Farm, and one of their daughters, Margaret, married Andrew Reid, farmer in Calliburn; they had seven children, whence the Reid families at Balliwilline and offshoots.[52]

10. **CLARK**. The death of Mary Clark, at the age of two, must have impressed itself deeply in the memory of the local community, and particularly its farming element, because I heard of it several times over the years, without, however, receiving any but the barest of particulars. The story is that Robert Clark, his wife Isabella, and their two children were returning by dogcart from Campbeltown to Glenehervie Farm by the Learside road on 7 February, 1913, a Friday (market day). At the Second Waters – where the road dips almost to sea-level at the stone bridge below Balnabraid Glen – the Clarks met John McIntyre, the farmer in neighbouring Feochaig, who was travelling in the same direction with his milk cart. The two men walked their horses up the steep brae at Corphin and remounted their vehicles at the top. Mrs Clark was seated on the left side of the cart, with Mary – her younger child – asleep on her lap, protected from the wind by an umbrella. The Clarks' horse had just begun trotting again, when the right wheel suddenly ran over an obstacle, throwing mother and child on to the road. Mrs Clark escaped serious injury, but Mary was killed instantly. The obstacle was later found to be a bag of feed which John McIntyre had tied at the back of his cart, and which had slipped off unnoticed.[53]

   This stone is one of three, side by side, to members of the Clark farming family, which descends through Robert Clark and Mary Galbraith, and Robert Clark and Catherine McNair (married 1861), who were parents of the tragic Mary's father, Robert,

Mary Clark

who married Isabella Watson on 4/8/1899.[54] As the inscription records, Isabella died on 18/6/1923, at the age of 52, and Robert on 5/3/1955, at the age of 93.

The surname Clark is recorded in Kintyre from the seventeenth century, becoming more common in the eighteenth. The Gaelic Clarks are sometimes represented by such forms as 'McInclerich', 'McA'Chlery', and 'McCleirach', for *Mac a' chleirich*, 'Son of the clerk'.

Division 2

11. **GRAHAM**. This is one of the many stones in Kilkerran which commemorate a life lost at sea. That there are many such losses recorded here is hardly surprising, given Campbeltown's former importance as both a trading and a fishing port, which in turn also made its seafaring population a natural recruitment source for naval service in times of war.

This stone records the death of Alexander Graham, son of Angus Graham and Mary Hunter, 'who perished in the wreck of the Hestia on Grand Manan Island, St. John's N.B., 25th Oct. 1909, & interred in the Mountain Cemetery, Yarmouth, Nova Scotia'. The Steam Ship *Hestia*, of the Donaldson Line, left Glasgow on 10 October for St. John, New Brunswick, with a crew of 35 and five passengers. The night of 25 October was stormy and thick with rain, and, an hour into his watch, helmsman William McCandless saw in the darkness ahead a form which he took to be an unlit schooner, but which turned out to be the Old Proprietor rock ledge, south-east of Grand Manan. At 1.10 a.m. the *Hestia* struck the ledge.

After some four hours aground, Captain Newman decided to abandon ship. The smaller of the lifeboats was launched with 11 men in her, but while she was still being lowered, a great sea caught and emptied her. Nine of them drowned, as did all 25 of those who took to the larger lifeboat, which grounded south of Yarmouth. Three corpses were entangled in the thwarts, and others began to wash ashore during the following days. In all,

Alexander Graham

30 men and four boys were lost, and the bells of the Yarmouth churches tolled as the funeral procession made its way to the graveyard.

Alexander Graham was among the dead. He had previously served on the yacht *Zara*, and was on his first trip with the *Hestia*, as second steward. He had been married for just over a year. William Hart, assistant steward, another of the dead, also had a Campbeltown connection. He was a son of Sergeant-Major Hart of the Argyllshire Rifles, formerly instructor to the Campbeltown companies and by then retired in Dunoon. Able Seaman Archibald Murray, son of Duncan Murray, Tarbert, also perished.

There were six survivors (two of whom had already survived the first launch). They had refused to leave the ship on the second lifeboat, and all six spent 38 harrowing hours, without food or water and lashed to the rigging of the battered *Hestia*, before being taken off. One of them was the third mate, Sam Stewart of Campbeltown, a son of the late James Stewart, owner and master of the local schooner *James Shearer*, which Sam had latterly commanded before she changed hands.

The *Hestia* was carrying one of the most valuable cargoes destined for St. John that year: carpets, fabrics, ropes, and – a grim irony – a quantity of tombstones, which strewed the rocks she struck on. In the 1970s, after three intact cases of whisky were salvaged from the wreck after more than 60 years on the seabed, 'historians were treated to a once in a lifetime taste of vintage Scotch'.[55]

Both Angus Graham and Mary Hunter died in Dunoon, he in 1902 at the age of 70, and she in 1910 at the age of 73. The family appears in the 1881 Census of Campbeltown. Angus was then a distillery maltman, born in Campbeltown, as were all his seven children; but Mary's birthplace is given as Islay. The locally unusual forename Adam – also associated with the Largieside McCorkindales and McPhails – recurs in this family.

The name Graham derives from the place-name Grantham in Lincolnshire and was introduced into Scotland early in the twelfth century by an Anglo-Norman family, de Graham.[56] Curiously, the related English surname Grantham is also represented in Kilkerran.[57] There are Grahams recorded in Kintyre in the eighteenth century, but the earlier form of the name here is McIlvernock[58] which represents Gaelic *Mac Gille Mhearnaig*, 'Son of the Servant of [Saint] Ernan'. The name Graham in Campbeltown can also have a nineteenth century origin in County Donegal, Ireland – see *Kintyre: The Hidden Past*, p 201 – where it may originally have been O *Goirmleadhaigh* (Gormley).[59]

12. **O'HARA**. The mid-nineteenth century was a time of extreme change and bitter conflict among the fishermen of Kintyre and Loch Fyneside, and this is the grave of one, John O'Hara, who lived through that time and was touched by its hardships.

For centuries there had been one dominant method of herring-fishing, the drift-net, but in the 1830s a cheaper and more efficient method began to find favour among some of the Tarbert fishermen. This was the 'trawl' – actually a beach seine-net – which evolved, with the coming of motor-power, into the ring-net: Kintyre's unique contribution to world fishing technology. Trawling was by no means universally welcomed, and from 1851 until 1867 was prohibited by law. Throughout that period, trawl crews were harassed ashore by fishery officers and by a special police force recruited in 1860, and at sea by a succession of gunboats. Nets and fishing skiffs were confiscated, many fishermen were jailed and two were shot, one fatally.[60]

In April 1861, my great-great grandfather, John Martin, and five of his Dalintober crew, including his son Duncan, were jailed for illegal fishing, a case which occupied eight column inches in the *Glasgow Herald* of 30 April 1861, and prompted a leader in that same newspaper the following day. The charge was not directly linked to trawling, though the link is obvious, but to a breach of the herring 'close time', a law, passed in 1860, which prohibited all herring fishing between Ardnamurchan in the north and the Mull of Galloway in the south between 1 January and 31 May. This detested legislation criminalised subsistence fishermen and the line-fishermen who depended on herring for bait, and was the cause of widespread hardship and suffering.

John O'Hara

John O'Hara was caught, almost a year on, in the same legal net. At Campbeltown New Quay, on 24 March 1862, James Low, fishery officer, noticed the skiff *Stork* 'carefully covered over with the sail'. Following a 'close examination', herring scales were found in the boat. Boat and gear were later claimed by James Martin, who explained the herring scales as being last season's, and maintained that the trawl was used only for catching 'cuddins' (small saithe). Low was sure that Martin and his associate, John O'Hara, had been fishing herring for line-bait, but the charge against them was subsequently found not proven, though the boat and two nets were declared forfeit.[61]

This James Martin was not one of the established local Martins (no. 31), but belonged to an Irish immigrant family from County Tyrone, which, outwith its genetic legacy, has disappeared here. John O'Hara was his brother-in-law, who had married Susanah or Susan Martin in 1856, and a brother of James O'Hara, who, in the previous year, had 'sailed for the East Indies' ahead of his prosecution in another illegal fishing case. The prospect of jail must surely have frightened him, but he did return to Campbeltown and married Ann Meenan in 1867, the year in which the repressive legislation was repealed.[62]

That previous prosecution arose from the sale of trawled herring to James McKinven, innkeeper at Carradale, in October 1861, and those jailed for 30 days were John's father Duncan O'Hara, born in County Antrim; William Davidson, born in County Tyrone; Alexander McLean; and James McCoag from Tarbert.[63] The herring, cured in 20 barrels, were forfeited at the trial, and several days later were carted away by Samuel Mitchell, farmer at Strath, to be spread as fertiliser, under the supervision of James Low. Soon after Low left, however, 'bands of women and children assembled in the field where the herrings were covered, and carried them away in considerable quantities to their homes'. Poverty, indeed; but at least the fish were judged to be 'of good quality'.[64]

The O'Haras were the pre-eminent fishing family of Irish origin in Campbeltown during the final half of the nineteenth century and were still represented among local boat-owners into the final half of the twentieth century, by Michael 'Mick' O'Hara, who had the *Nan McMurrar* built in 1946 and the *Anne Philomena* built in 1948, both at Peterhead. The last individual of the name in Campbeltown was Henry O'Hara, who died at the age of 72 on 17/9/2006. An account of the once extensive O'Hara family, and its intermarriages with other Irish immigrant families, appears in my *Kintyre: The Hidden Past*, pp. 205-6.

On 23 January 1872, Susan O'Hara, suffering from typhoid fever, was admitted to the Poorhouse in Campbeltown and remained there until 1 February. Her husband John was unable to assist her, being 'from home, a fisherman'. She was then aged 34, described as a fishwife, and had five children: James, Mary, Duncan, John and Henry, the youngest at one year.[65] On 18/2/1896, Henry married Vincent Ceni Celetti Durnin, whose curious forenames are explained on p 64 of *An Historical and Genealogical Tour of Kilkerran Graveyard*. John O'Hara died on 11/9/1905, aged 68, and Susanah on 25/9/1884, aged 49.

The name in Irish is *O hEaghra*, 'Descendant of Eaghra',

who was a chief of Leyna in County Sligo, whence a branch of the family migrated, in the fourteenth century, to the Glens of Antrim,[66] where, at Cushendun, *circa* 1806, the progenitor of the Campbeltown O'Haras, Duncan, was born.

13. **McNEILAGE**.   This is one of the many surnames which were well known in Kintyre by the nineteenth century, but disappeared in the twentieth.   Despite a superficial resemblance, the name is not connected with the old Kintyre name MacNeill, but is a corrupt form of McNelis, from Gaelic *Mac Niallghuis*, which translates as 'Son of Champion Choice'.[67]   Farmers of the name are recorded in 1692 – Donald mc neilledge in Glensadell, and John mc neilledge and George mc neilladge in Kilmacho and Langa[68] – and in 1694 Donald appears again, more specifically in Mains of Saddell, along with Archibald McNeilladge in Aross.[69] In the census of 1792, which was restricted to the Duke of Argyll's properties in Kintyre, no fewer than 24 individuals of the name are indexed.[70]

This sandstone monument, which is eroding badly, was raised by Malcolm McNeilage to his wife Agnes Galbraith, who died of tuberculosis at the age of 23 on 28/10/1886.   He describes himself as of 'Durban, Natal', which suggests that he emigrated to South Africa after his wife's death, but little else is known about him.   He was a son of Archibald McNeilage, tailor in Dalintober, and Catherine McIntosh, and a grandson of Donald/ Daniel MacNeillage, weaver, Lochend, and Stewart MacPhail, who married on 27/8/1799.[71]   'Stewart' as a female forename is unusual.   Archibald named one of his daughters 'Stewart', after his mother, as did – spelling 'Stuart' – Archibald's brother Malcolm, a merchant in Campbeltown who married Margaret Beith and is buried with her in the old section of Kilkerran.

In 'A Macneilage Family of Campbeltown', published in the *Kintyre Magazine*, author and historian Enid Gauldie tells the story of her father, William Macneilage, and of his father, David, a brother of the Malcolm who raised this stone.   David qualified as a doctor and attended his sister-in-law, Agnes, during her terminal illness.   He ended his medical career in Manchester and died there in 1907. William was born in County Durham in 1878, but spent his boyhood in Campbeltown. His mother, Agnes McAdam, had died, and life with his stepmother was unhappy. At the age of 15, he ran away to sea.[72] Another son of Dr Macneilage's, Archibald – 'an old Grammar School boy' – set out his impressions of the Boer War in a letter published in the *Argyllshire Herald* of 20/1/1900. A Dalintober fisherman, John McNeilage, drowned when he fell overboard from the skiff *Bella* during ring-netting operations off Drumadoon, Arran, on the opening day of the 1903 summer herring-fishing season, 1 June. He was about 30 years old and unmarried[73], and was one of the last of the name in Kintyre.

Division 5

14. **McCALLUM.** This name – from Gaelic *Mac Ghille Chaluim*, 'Devotee of Saint Columba' – has already been examined in my *An Historical and Genealogical Tour of Kilkerran Graveyard*. This McCallum, Malcolm, was born in Greenock, but his family origin was Tarbert, Loch Fyne. MG McCallum ARCO LRAM, came to Campbeltown in 1933 as music master at Campbeltown Grammar School and in the same year was appointed conductor of Campbeltown Gaelic Choir. His association with that celebrated choir was to last 27 years and provide him with many of the peaks of his musical career. In 1954, at the Edinburgh Festival, the choir performed for an entire week in 'Hail Caledonia', a show compered by the late Roddy Macmillan; in 1958, when Queen Elizabeth and the Duke of Edinburgh visited Campbeltown, Malcolm conducted the choir in front of them; and in 1960 – the year before he died, at the age of 58 – he was with the choir when it won the prestigious Lovat and Tullibardine Trophy at the National Mod for the 13th time, a record which no other choir or conductor has ever surpassed.

Gaelic Choir.   Malcolm McCallum   '09.

He was organist and choirmaster of Lochend United Free Church – demolished in 1990 and the site cleared to form a supermarket car-park – and also an elder. He also made his musical talents available to country choirs, including those of the Scottish Women's Rural Institute, which seems remarkable now that these admirable groups – once bastions of traditional home-baking and educational entertainment – are so reduced in branches and membership. The Kintyre Music Club, which continues to thrive, also benefited by his membership; he was a former chairman and a committee member at the time of his death. Outwith music, his main interests lay in civic service. He was a member of Campbeltown Town Council from 1945 until his death, serving as Bailie and Convener of the Parks Committee. A keen member and past President of Campbeltown Bowling Club, he spent much of his leisure on the bowling-green at Stronvaar.

He was survived by his wife Annie G Bennie, who died on 18/11/1976, aged 68, and by two sons, Calum and Raibeart

(Robert), who is a singer and a past conductor of the Glasgow Hebridean Gaelic Choir, which he founded, and from whom much of the above information was received. Annie was born in Scotstoun, but came to Campbeltown at six weeks old. Her father, Robert Bennie, was foreman joiner at Trench Point Shipyard and is buried in Division 3.

It was Malcolm McCallum who set to music the lovely poem by Latimer McInnes, 'Nostalgia', which was written in Rome, and of which this is the first verse.

But oh! my heart is weary, very weary here afar,
For the grey reach of Kilbrannan when the spindrift's flying free,
For the mist-swathed peaks of Arran and the sight of green
      Davaar
As the screw goes throbbing homeward to the place where
      I would be;
Oh! to ramble through the Plantin, to bask in Porter's Glen,
To wade knee-deep in bracken on dear old Harvey's Braes,
To sit on black McRinnans and watch the fishermen
Go seaward through the sunset or homeward through the haze.

The poem has a curious history. A 'dirty and rejected' manuscript copy was purportedly found in 1922 in the town rubbish-dump at Gortan and published as a curiosity in the *Campbeltown Courier*.[74] Latimer McInnes appears not to have acknowledged his authorship, publicly at any rate, and the version which he included in his privately published *Poems* of 1942 is almost identical to the one he presumably discarded with his rubbish 20 years earlier. But the original title, 'Ceannloch', he changed to 'Nostalgia', and he replaced the final line in verse two, 'I have wet my limbs in Tiber and laved my face in Po', with, 'I have learned in pictured Florence all an artist longs to know'. No great critical acumen is required, I feel, to explain what lay behind that line's ultimate rejection. Though his reference is obviously to the River Po, a 'po' is also a piss-pot, and the comic potential must have struck him later. Raibeart McCallum has a copy of McInnes's *Poems*, inscribed to his father by the author, the only copy outwith Campbeltown Public Library of which I am aware.

15. **SPEED**. This is one of those names – Wareham is another – which were so familiar in Campbeltown that one scarcely noticed their essential incongruity: they sounded very English in the mix of Gaelic, Irish and Scots names which made up the population of south Kintyre in the last century. Wareham, indeed, is English[75], but the name Speed is not so easily explained. I remember the late Tom Speed telling me in 1978 that the first of the family was an Estonian fisherman who 'came up the quay in clogs'; and Tom's cousin, Malcolm Speed, was told that it was a Dutchman who 'walked around Campbeltown in his clogs'!

Speed is predominantly an English surname, but also appears in Scottish records. The key figure in the family's establishment in the Campbeltown fishing community is Matthew Speed, a fisherman who died on 22/10/1900 at the age of 49 in Shore Street. He was twice married: to Mary Blair and then to Janet Wareham, both of them from local fishing families. His parents were Alexander Speed, hotel keeper, and Mary McPhail, who married in Glasgow on 15/11/1853.

The Speed family emerged later than most as boat-owners. The ring-netter *Moira* was built by Walter Reekie, St Monans, in 1949, for the brothers Matthew and Neil, whose father, Seaman-Gunner Malcolm Blair Speed, had been lost at sea (on 24/2/1918) during the First World War.[76] By the time the *Moira* was sold to Lybster, in 1967, both brothers were dead.

Neil McLean Speed DSM – commemorated on this stone – was the first to die, in 1954. An act of singular bravery during the evacuation of British troops from Dunkirk, in 1940, earned him his Distinguished Service Medal. He was Coxswain on the paddle minesweeper *Gracie Fields* which, during the dawn of 29 May, under a constant hail of bombs, shells and bullets, lifted no fewer than 900 troops from the beaches. Then a bomb struck the vessel amidships and wiped out the entire engine-room crew, killing and wounding many others. With the main steam-pipe shattered by the explosion, her boilers threatening to burst and the hundreds of survivors in imminent danger of being scalded to death, Neil dashed through the clouds of steam, disappeared below into 'terrible danger', and managed to shut off the steam.

Having reappeared on deck, he remarked coolly: 'It's all right, boys – don't worry.'[77] Neil later served under the legendary U-boat hunter, Captain Frederick 'Johnny' Walker, CB and four times DSO, about which posting Tom Ralston, in his memoir *My Captains*, has a memorable story to tell.[78]

On the night of his death, on 16/4/1954, Neil, accompanied by his half-brother Robert McMillan, had gone down Campbeltown Old Quay to check the engine of the *Moira*, which he skippered. While climbing ashore from the boat, Neil collapsed and fell into the harbour. He was recovered from the water by police officers on night duty, but was 'beyond aid'. He was 42 years old.[79] His widow, Mary Thomson, was 86 when she died on 24/7/1999.

As though his wartime exploits were not enough, Neil was also involved in the dramatic rescue of the *Mobeka*'s crew in 1942 (no. 19). He was home on leave from the Navy at the time of the call-out, and received, for his part in the rescue, the Royal National Lifeboat Institution's bronze medal and parchment. The lifeboat coxswain on that night was Neil's father-in-law, James Thomson.

Neil's brother, Matthew, also served throughout the Second World War, on minesweepers, and was 47 years old when he died at sea aboard the *Moira* on 30/4/1958. His widow, Euphemia Gilchrist, lived to the age of 92 and died on 6/5/2001. Their son, Malcolm Blair Speed, had a distinguished career in Scottish journalism. He got his start in 1957 as junior reporter on the *Campbeltown Courier*, then moved to the *Airdrie & Coatbridge Advertiser*, of which he became Editor shortly before his 22nd birthday. In 1965 he joined the *Scottish Daily Mail* as a reporter, and in 1966 moved to the *Daily Record*, returning to Campbeltown in May of that year to cover the sinking of the pleasure cruiser *Quesada*, in which his school friend John Paterson was one of those who drowned. One of his last working trips to Campbeltown was to interview Paul and Linda McCartney at High Park Farm. In 1971 he became an executive on the *Daily Record*, was promoted to News Editor in 1983, and was further promoted, in 1994, to the role of Managing Editor of both the *Record* and *Sunday Mail*, which post he held until his retirement in October 2006.[80]

16. **TAYLOR.** Although commemorated in the 6th Division – the most recent, and final, extension of Kilkerran Cemetery – Leslie Arthur Taylor's death predates its utilisation. As his inscription shows, he was one of 862 fatalities when the battleship HMS *Barham* was torpedoed on 25/11/1941 in the Eastern Mediterranean. Operating out of Alexandria with the Mediterranean Fleet, she was engaged in hunting Italian convoys to Libya, when, north of Sidi Barrani, U-331 – commanded by Hans-Dietrich Frieherr von Tiesenhausen – fired a spread of four torpedoes towards her. Three of them struck her port side, causing her to list heavily and spreading fire. Within three minutes, HMS *Barham* had rolled on to her side and her after magazine had exploded with spectacular effect (captured on film, and the images much used in books and films). Despite the appearance of total catastrophe conveyed by these photographs, some 450 of her crew survived. Sergeant Leslie Taylor, Royal Marines, was not, however, one of the survivors. U-331 eluded retribution and arrived back at Salamis, Greece, on 21/2/1942.

Tiesenhausen, her captain, recounted in 1998 that he had spotted a group of three British battleships, flanked by eight destroyers. At periscope depth, he eased U-331 between two of the destroyers and fired at the middle battleship in the line. The release of weight brought the U-boat's bow shooting to the surface, and her conning-tower, too, lifted clear, barely 150 yards ahead of the third battleship in the line, HMS *Valiant*. Her captain immediately altered course, in a wide arc, and bore down on U-331, intending to ram her; but her engineers got her under just in time. During her descent, the depth-gauge needle inexplicably slowed and then stopped at 250 ft.; but her crew sensed that she was still in motion, and a mood of deep unease prevailed, because the maximum safe depth was reckoned to be 330 ft. When Tiesenhausen requested that a second, forward, gauge be consulted, the reading – an unprecedented 820 ft. – appalled the crew. As the dive was frantically reversed and

U-331 began to ascend, her hull, which theoretically should have been crushed, did not as much as spring a leak.[81]

H.M.S. Barham exploding (drawn from an original photograph)

Sgt Leslie Taylor

The sinking of the *Barham* generated a further remarkable story, that of Helen Duncan, the spiritist medium born in Callander, Perthshire, in 1897. During the Second World War she was living in Portsmouth, where in 1941 'she spoke with a deceased sailor from HMS *Barham*' and revealed that the ship had been sunk in the Mediterranean, information which had not then been officially released. Her activities increasingly attracted the attention of the authorities, and on 19 January, 1944, she and three members of her audience were arrested during a seance. She was subsequently charged under the Witchcraft Act of 1735, and sentenced to nine months' imprisonment, so becoming the last convicted Scottish 'witch'.[82]

As a rule, news of local casualties and prisoners of war was reported quite promptly in the *Campbeltown Courier*, but not a word on Sergeant Taylor and his loss in the *Barham* appeared in its pages, aside from a public intimation, almost a month later, revealing only that he had died 'on Active Service on the 25th November, 1941'. In February 1943, however, it was reported that Sergeant Taylor's widow had attended a special commemorative service in Westminster Abbey .[83]

There were many marriages during the Second World War between Campbeltown women and servicemen based here, but this was not one of them. The story of Jean Bell and Leslie's meeting, preserved in family tradition, is a romantic one. His ship was anchored in Campbeltown Loch and he was ashore with shipmates. Jean was strolling by the Picture House with two cousins, and, as Leslie passed, he indicated her and remarked: 'That's the girl I'm going to marry.' They were married in 1929 at Moy Villa, the house of Jean's sister Barbara, Mrs Alistair McMillan. The wedding party travelled there and back by the 'Wee Train'.

Leslie Taylor was born in Romford, Essex, in 1906 – son of Edward Arthur Taylor, a butcher – but brought up in Rainham. Leslie and Jean had three daughters, separated in age by 10 years: Margaret, who married James Robertson (both buried in the Taylor lair); then Kathleen Anne (Mrs Charles McKechnie); and finally Norma, who married a Tarbert fisherman – later joiner – James McDougall, and lived there before they moved to Irvine, Ayrshire.[84]

Though a thin scattering of Bells appears in Kintyre records during the nineteenth century, mainly in the north of the peninsula, the Bell families in Campbeltown seem to descend from Angus Bell, who was born in Bowmore, Islay. His wife was Agnes Paterson, Southend, and they had four surviving children – Neil, Mary, Archibald, and Duncan – in 1880, the year of Angus's death at the age of 70. All the sons at that time were fishermen, and Mary's husband, Neil McMillan, was also a fisherman.[85] Jean Taylor's parents were Archibald Bell and Margaret McMichael Mason. The Mason family in Campbeltown stems from William Mason, who was born in Glasgow, married Jeannie Brown of Campbeltown – parents John Brown, butcher, and Margaret McMichael – on 25/11/1891, and worked in Benmore Distillery.[86]

17. **BOYLE**. This is the grave of my maternal grandmother, Barbara Boyle. Both stone and inscription are economical; a compromise, since some of the family maintained that she had not wanted a monument. That she had a difficult life is certain. Her father, John Boyle, was a violent drunkard. His father, also John Boyle, was Irish, and John Jnr. appears to have been brought up in Dublin; but his mother Amelia McKerral was of Learside stock, and John Jnr. came to Campbeltown as a young man to serve an apprenticeship as a plater at Campbeltown Shipyard. One of the directors of the Campbeltown Shipbuilding Company, Donald MacKay – see *An Historical and Genealogical Tour of Kilkerran Graveyard*, p 44 – was John's first cousin once removed, and family tradition avers that, in other circumstances, John might have advanced himself at the yard.

He met and married a Campbeltown girl, Barbara Thomson, whose father, Dugald Thomson, a fisherman, had come to Campbeltown from Skipness and married Agnes McCallum in 1859. They had four surviving children, of whom Barbara – born on 16/6/1865, at New Quay Head – was the youngest. On John Boyle's wage, life should have been comfortable enough for Barbara and her children, but his habit was to spend the contents of his wage-packet before she even saw it. She died in childbed in 1902 at the age of 37, and on her eldest daughter Amelia fell the burden of raising an impoverished family. My grandmother remembered thinning turnips as a child, and her sisters Agnes and Margaret would be sent to the quay for fish when the boats came in. Their uncle, Donald Thomson, was a fisherman and boat-owner, and his generosity could no doubt be relied upon, though he and his wife Margaret Calderwood themselves had 14 children. The family later moved to Glasgow to escape their father's attentions, but he followed them there and was turned away from their door. As a consequence of their experiences with an alcoholic father, few of John Boyle's family tolerated alcohol when they grew up. Amelia's fiance, Alex Rankin, had a long wait until he was able to marry her, and they had no children – she said that she had already brought up a family.

John Boyle apparently came into a substantial inheritance late in life. His daughter Agnes maintained that he drank away most of the money and that there was barely the sum of £80 apiece left to his children. 'He took too long to drink himself into the grave,' she would complain. A letter written by John's sister, Jane, in 1930, hints at this legacy, when she remarks that her mother 'was left money from a Mrs Barbara Reid' (a daughter of Neil McKerral, Brunerican). This sister, Mrs Jane Carcary, of Castlepollard, County Westmeath, Ireland, was, in 1930, on the track of another, unclaimed legacy, but the rest of her generation, including her husband Donald and brother John, were all dead. That legacy was apparently still unclaimed in 1941, by which time Jane had been involved with at least two American lawyers in her efforts to secure the money, or at least a share of it.

Her claim was founded, of course, on ties of kinship, and to that end she contacted Mr Archibald MacKay, farmer at Lephenstrath, Southend, who was himself a relative. The key figure in the genealogical puzzle was one Ellen McKerral, who was born in 1821 and married Hugh Mathieson. Ellen was a daughter of Neil McKerral and Barbara McEachran. Her brother John, born in Kilmashenachan in 1810, married Amelia McKay, born at Erradil in 1806, and they were grandparents of Jane Carcary. Hugh Mathieson also belonged to a Southend family, Duncan McMath or Mathieson and Mary Fleming, in Machribeg, being his parents. Hugh Mathieson and family appear to have gone to Campbeltown, where he found work as a maltster in a distillery, then migrated to Londonderry around 1860, after which they disappeared, presumably to America.

Whether or not her claim succeeded remains unknown, but the flurry of correspondence it generated – involving, among others, Archie McEachran, Kilblaan, a noted Southend historian – yielded genealogical expositions which owe as much to oral tradition as to documentary sources, and which could scarcely be compiled now with such assurance. The following extract, from notes written by Archie McEachran in 1941, provides an example of the kind of complexities so deftly expressed: ' It may interest Mrs Carcary to know also that her grandparents

John McKerral and Amelia McKay were presumably second cousins. His grandfather was old Hugh McKerral in Balnabraid (afterwards in Brunerican) and Amelia McKay's mother, Margt McKerral, was a daughter of another of the Balnabraid McKerrals, possibly Peter, whose wife was Janet Gilchrist.'

With the exception of my grandmother, none of the children of John Boyle and Barbara Thomson – Amelia McKerral McKay (1884-1964), Agnes McCallum (1888-1975), Barbara (1890-1978) Marion Thomson (1892-1979), John (1894-1966), Margaret Wilson (1896-1982), Dougald (1898-1972) and Jean (1902-1975) – returned to Campbeltown, other than on holidays. A son of Dougald Boyle and Nan McPhail, Professor Iain Thomson Boyle DSc, BSc (Hons), MB, ChB, FRCP (Glasgow, London) distinguished himself in the medical profession as a specialist in metabolic bone diseases. He died in 2001.

Barbara Boyle was in domestic service in Glasgow until her marriage to John McKenzie in 1911. He was in the Seaforth Highlanders in the First World War and was killed at Passchendaele in 1917. Barbara was left with three children, James, Amelia – my mother – and John. Barbara's second husband, George Moffat, survived the war, but suffered for the rest of his life the effects of a bayonet wound to the elbow. George and Barbara had two sons, George and Dugald. George, a navigator in the RAF, was lost in 1940, when shot down. Barbara Moffat returned to Campbeltown in her second widowhood and died there on 25/6/1978 at the age of 88.[87]

Division 3

18. **McBRIDE**. MacBride can be either Irish or Scottish Gaelic and represents *Mac Gille Brighde*, Son of the Servant of (Saint) Bridget, though the name *Bridghe* was probably originally attached to a pre-Christian fire-goddess, many of whose attributes were later transferred to the historical figure of Saint Brigit of Kildare (452-523), founder of the first Irish convent.[88] Outwith nineteenth century Irish immigrants and the Traveller

community – Townsley families, in particular – the name Bridget was not favoured locally.

The William McBride commemorated here belonged to Arran. His parents, William McBride and Ann Lamb, were, however, born in Ayrshire, though it is a possibility that the family was originally an Arran one. GF Black describes MacBride as 'an old name on Arran', and also, in relation to both Arran and Kintyre, examines its pet or diminutive form MacBridan (Gaelic *Mac Bhridein*).[89] MacBridan/MacBride was well represented in north Kintyre from the seventeenth century through to the nineteenth, early examples being John mc Bridane in Tangintavill and Lagalgeirve, and Archibald mc Bridaine in Killocra and Corilich, in 1692[90], and Donald and Peter MacBride in Achaluskin and Balergus, respectively, in 1797.[91] Daniel McBride, Campbeltown, was drowned from the smack *Brilliant* in Kilbrannan Sound in 1862.[92]

This headstone was erected by William McBride to his wife Isabella Martin, who was my grandfather's sister, and to two of their children who predeceased her. Like many others in my family who disappeared early by death or dispersal, a few doubtful stories cling to Bella's memory. One such is that she used to return to Dalintober from Arran to have her babies, and so much enjoyed being back among her own family that her husband invariably had to sail back across and take her away. The Census of 1901 certainly has all of her children up until then – Sarah, John, Annie and Lawrence – born in Campbeltown, but the family, her husband included, was not in Pirnmill, but in McInnes's Land, North Shore Street, Dalintober.

When her son William Wilson died at the age of three in 1896, he died at Queen Street, Dalintober. When her 13-year-old daughter Sarah Campbell died in 1908, she died in Princes Street, Dalintober. And when Isabella herself died in 1909, she too was in Princes Street.[93] Even more significantly, when Willie McBride's skiffs, the *Annie* and the *Ella*, were launched in the summer of 1912 from Munro's boatyard at Ardrishaig, they were brought not to Arran – though registered 'GK' for Greenock, the Arran port of registry – but to Campbeltown.[94] The evidence strongly suggests that Willie and Bella McBride lived for the greater part of their marriage, if not for their entire marriage, in Dalintober, and that Willie remained there for three years after his wife's death.

Isabella was 39 years old when she died. According to another family tradition, her death, in or shortly after childbirth, so embittered her brothers against Willie McBride that they 'chased him away'. The inference was that she had some medical condition which rendered further child-bearing dangerous, and that Willie had been 'warned to have no more'. Isabella's death certificate disposes indisputably of that one: she died of cancer of the stomach.[95]

It is therefore improbable, in the extreme, that poor Willie – a successful and respected fisherman – was 'chased away'; but that he went away is certain, for his and Isabella's surviving children were brought up in Pirnmill, Arran, and the boys – Jackie, Lawrence and Angus – followed their father to the fishing. Willie married again – to Christina McLeod from Polbain, Achiltibuie, Wester Ross, in 1913 – but his expressed desire was to be buried with Bella, and his body was returned in April 1937 and laid beside her body, where they'd buried two of their children, Willie and Sarah.

The McBride family in Carradale was founded by a brother of Willie's, Lawrence, and his wife Helen Sharp, who belonged to Longriggend, Airdrie, and whom he met while she was at Pirnmill in service with a family on holiday there. According to McBride family tradition, when Lawrence – also a fisherman and boat-owner – wished to build a house at Pirnmill, he was unable to obtain a plot of land there, so he built instead at Port na Cuile, Carradale.[96]

The sculptor John MacBride (1819-90) was a son of Archibald MacBride of Campbeltown.[97]

19. **LAMBRECHT, GONZALES, VANBESIEN**. This pink sandstone memorial, on the north side of the stream which flows through the graveyard, marks the graves of five Belgian fishermen – the brothers Marcel, Henri and Frans Lambrecht, David Gonzales and Frans Vanbesien – who died in a double

shipwreck off Southend during the Second World War. Both their little wooden fishing vessel, the *Annie Marie* (O 349), and the 426 ft.-long steel-built *Mobeka*, ran aground and were wrecked on the same morning and in the same place; but the most remarkable coincidence in this story is that both vessels belonged to Belgium.

In mid-1941, Marcel Lambrecht and his crew escaped from German-occupied Belgium in the *Annie Marie*, and continued fishing in British waters. When the Ostend-registered trawler ran aground at 7.45 a.m. on Monday, 19 January 1942, her skipper fired off distress flares. These were seen, and at 7.53 Southend Coastguard notified the RNLI in Campbeltown. Just before the lifeboat was launched, another message was received from Southend, that a second vessel had grounded off Carskey, but in a more westerly position. This was the *Mobeka*, which had set out from Liverpool on the previous day to join a convoy through the North Channel and then proceed south to West Africa.

When the Coastguard team arrived at Carskey, they found the *Annie Marie* aground at the extremity of a reef and being pounded by heavy seas in a south-easterly gale. Although a breeches-buoy rocket-line did reach the crew, they failed to haul it in. Perhaps they had little understanding of how the life-saving apparatus worked; there were language difficulties, too; and they were surely numbed by wind, sleet and spray. At 10.20, the rescue team saw, with horror, that two of the fishermen had slung the rocket-line round their waists and jumped into the sea. The Coastguards pulled them ashore on the flimsy line, and three of their crewmates plunged into the sea after them and were washed ashore. All five were given artificial respiration, but only one regained consciousness. A sixth crewman had earlier been washed overboard and drowned. The sole survivor was a young boy – name unknown – who was given accommodation and employment for about a year by Mrs Winifred Parsons of Carskey Estate, but drowned later in the war. The lair and headstone in Kilkerran were paid for by the Campbeltown branch of the charitable organisation, the St Vincent de Paul Society.[98]

Lambrecht, Gonzales, Vanbesien

By around 11 a.m., Southend Coastguard had shifted position and hailed the *Mobeka*'s master, Captain Lauwereins, asking him what assistance he required. He replied that he wished to land four passengers and some of his crew. A raft, with three seamen and an officer on board, was almost smashed to bits but reached shore at about 11.35, followed by the passengers and two crewmen in a small boat, aided by the Coastguards' life-saving gear.

The Campbeltown lifeboat, *Duke of Connaught* – on temporary duty at the station – arrived at the *Mobeka* at 12.15 p.m., having had her rudder damaged on passage. Added to that handicap, the force of wind and sea was still increasing, and sleet and snow thickening. The lifeboat coxswain, James Thomson, realising that it would be suicidal to run his vessel alongside the *Mobeka*, therefore anchored to windward and by slipping the cable was able to manoeuvre around the stern of the lurching ship and into the relative shelter of her hull. The lifeboat's engine then began to malfunction, but Coxswain Thomson kept her alongside until the remaining crewmen – 44 in all, including Captain Lauwereins – were safely aboard. Four miles into the passage back to Campbeltown, the *Duke of Connaught*'s engine failed, was restarted and failed again. She ended up running into Dunaverty Bay under sail and landing the *Mobeka*'s crew at the old lifeboat slip there, whence they were taken to Campbeltown by road. These operations were completed without loss of life.

Attempts at salvaging the *Mobeka* failed and she became a total wreck. She was adjudged a war loss and her insured value was paid to her owners in 1944; but the *Annie Marie* was not so adjudged, and it took until 1949, after protracted dealings with insurance agents, before her owner's widow received a settlement. The unfortunate Captain Lauwereins failed to see the end of that traumatic year, for on 16 December 1942, as chief officer of the *Emile Francqui*, he perished at sea. One author who has analysed the evidence of the *Mobeka*'s grounding is certain that navigational error was the cause; but so far no one has identified with certainty the factors which caused that error,[99] though Moir and Crawford in *Argyll Shipwrecks* maintain that the *Mobeka*'s captain mistook the *Annie Marie*'s distress flares 'for a signal to join the convoy'.[100]

This account began with a coincidence – two Belgian vessels grounding on the same day and in the same place – and will end with a coincidence. Marceline Steinkiste, who for many years lived in Campbeltown as Mrs Alex McLellan, was related to one of the drowned fisherman, Frans Vanbesien: he was her mother's cousin. Her parents knew all the men who drowned, and, when visiting Marceline, always found time to visit Kilkerran Cemetery and pay their respects to the memory of their five countrymen who died far from home on that terrible morning.[101]

20. **DURNIN.** This name represents *O Doirnain* in Irish. There is one other form, Durnan, current in Campbeltown. Two Irishmen of the name, Michael and John, settled in Campbeltown in the first half of the nineteenth century. Since both were from County Fermanagh, they were probably related, but see my *Kintyre: The Hidden Past*, pp. 200-1, for a more detailed genealogical

examination. Michael, who arrived in Campbeltown *circa* 1836 with his wife Catherine Ward and three Fermanagh-born children, appears to be the more interesting of the two, as his obituary (1875) shows.

Michael Durnan died in his house in Shore Street on Sunday morning last, having attained the ripe age of eighty-nine. He was born in Ireland about 1785, and when a young man he joined the army and served for a number of years, retiring at the age of 31 in 1816, the year after the Battle of Waterloo, upon the pensioners' list.

During the time he served as a soldier he took part in the Peninsular War, that memorable era in English (*sic*) history, and was at the famous victory of Salamanca, under Wellington, against the French in 1812, and in other important engagements, and he obtained a medal dated 1848 for services in the British Army to 1816.

He retired a wounded soldier, having been shot in his right arm and right foot. Until shortly before his death he could speak clearly and descriptively of the various engagements, his countenance lighting up as he recalled the glorious victories in battle. Through the kindness of the Rev. Mr Russell he was enabled to obtain the increased pension granted to those who served at and before Waterloo, but at the time of his death he had participated in only two of these increased payments. He was the oldest soldier in town, and whenever able for work was industriously employed.[102]

Charles Durnin, who is buried here, was a son of the other immigrant, John, by his second wife Eliza Bonner, born at Pans (Machrihanish) in 1823, daughter of James Bonner, glazier. John was born *circa* 1811* in the parish of 'Macheramonagh', County Fermanagh, to Patrick Durnan – like Michael above, a soldier – and Catherine McGuire. His first wife, Bridget Stephen, also Irish-born, died c 1854 in Kirk Street. He remarried in 1861, and in 1877 was admitted to the Poorhouse in Campbeltown as homeless.[103]

Charles, who was born in 1862, became a fisherman and

married Janet Mathieson, after whom he named his first boat; his next was the *Osprey*, followed by the *Bluebird* in 1926. She was a 48-ft. East Coast Fifie, which three of his sons, Charles, James and John, fished[104] after his retirement, in 1931, owing to increasing blindness. Charles, according to his obituarist, went to sea at the age of 11, 'when he sailed north in a small coal vessel', and remembered sailing to Skipness and Cour, where the crews lived ashore in huts and tents during the day and fished at night.[105]

Probably his most memorable experience at sea, however, was on a winter's day when he almost died after an hour in the water. He was associated for many years with Southend lifeboat – launched from Dunaverty slip and crewed by Campbeltown fishermen – and by 1906 was her second coxswain. The lifeboat's quarterly exercise had been arranged for the last Friday of November 1906, and despite stormy conditions the crew agreed to go ahead. The lifeboat was crossing the wind through Dunaverty Bay on her first tack when Coxswain Henry O'Hara noticed a 'tremendous sea' approaching and 'immediately sang out to the crew to hold fast by the life-lines'.

The boat capsized and three of her crew, Charles Durnin, Andrew Mathieson and Archibald Mathieson, were thrown overboard. After several minutes of 'confusion and fear', while the boat 'spun round like a top, still on her side', she righted herself. The two Mathiesons were able regain the safety of the lifeboat, but by then Charles Durnin was out of reach. Fortunately for him, he was wearing a life-jacket, otherwise, encumbered as he was by sea-boots and oilskins, he could not have survived. 'As it was, the waves were completely breaking over him, and often he was completely lost to the sight of the crew. All were labouring under a great strain of anxiety for their comrade's fate, and the situation must have been exceedingly painful to his son [Charles Jnr.] who was also in the crew.' Durnin then got into broken water near a reef opposite Keil, where no boat could risk going, and the crew decided to return the lifeboat to the slip and attempt a rescue from the shore. That done, they ran across the sand to Keil, by which time Durnin was seen to be 'getting clear of the reef on which it was feared he might be dashed ... swimming a little, and thus guiding his course'.

Charles
Durnin

Some villagers, including James Taylor, had by this time arrived on the shore. Several of them and several lifeboatmen entered the surf to try to reach Durnin, but were almost carried off their feet. A rope was fetched from Keil House and tied around Taylor, 'whose inches stood him in good stead for entering the surf'. Twice Durnin was 'borne shorewards on the crest of a breaker, only to be dragged back to sea by the backwash', but with the third breaker Taylor managed to seize hold of him and both were hauled ashore on the end of the rope. Durnin was unconscious by then, but revived sufficiently to be taken to the hotel and cared for until fit, that evening, to be driven back to town. He recovered well, and, when interviewed, remarked that when he saw the lifeboat returning to the slip, he 'almost lost heart, thinking for the moment that his comrades were leaving him to his fate'. Another bout of despair occurred when he was being swept towards the reef at Keil; but it was a current which carried him to safer waters and 'not his own exertions'.[106] He lived to celebrate his golden and diamond wedding anniversaries, and, when he died on 25/6/1948, was survived by four sons and four daughters.[107]

Given his wife's history of tragedy, Charles Durnin's narrow escape from death by drowning was perhaps against the odds. Janet Mathieson's father, Dugald, was master of the Campbeltown smack *Mystery* which foundered on Skerryvore reef, Machrihanish, in May 1869, and he drowned at the age of 41 with all his crew. Her older sister, Mary, lost her husband, Hugh Robertson, when the Campbeltown schooner *Moy* foundered in 1884.[108]

* In my *Kintyre:The Hidden Past*, p 200, I estimated John's year of birth as having been 1791, but, by comparing two main sources and 'splitting the difference', 1811 appears to be a closer estimate.

21. **EAGLESOME**. This is an unusual variant of an unusual name. GF Black derives it from 'the old barony of Eaglesham in Renfrewshire', and cites James Paterson – *History of the Counties of Ayr and Wigton* (1863-66) – who refers to 'Eglesame' as 'an old surname in the parish of Ballantrae'.[109] From Ballantrae, indeed, came Thomas Eaglesham – as the name appears in the Census of 1861 – a salmon-fisherman at Peninver. He, however, is buried not in Kilkerran, but in Kilchousland – closer to his adopted home – along with his Dumfries-born wife, Elizabeth Graham, who survived him and died at Prestwick on 9/4/1900, and three sons who predeceased him.

Thomas Eaglesome came to Kintyre around 1850 and for the rest of his life lived in Peninver, first in a cottage and then in a more substantial building, erected in 1885[110] and known as Craiglussa. For the greater part of that period, he had the lease of the salmon-fishing rights at Peninver and prospered there. 'He was greatly above the average in intelligence, and could express shrewd opinions on most subjects,' his obituarist in the *Argyllshire Herald* remarked. 'Among those who liked to talk to him and listen to his sturdy good sense was his Grace the Duke of Argyll, who was never in the district without driving to the pretty cottage at Peninver and having a friendly chat with his old tenant.'[111] Thomas died suddenly on 9/11/1893 at the age of 76.

Eaglesomes have long since disappeared from Kintyre, but the name survives on one of the most attractive, and least altered, shop-fronts in Campbeltown, at Reform Square. This business, which since 2006 has largely been a hot and cold 'take-away', took its name from Thomas Eaglesome Jnr., who was apprenticed to William Dickson, 'Italian Warehouseman', in Reform Square. After four years in his employment, and at the age of only 18, Thomas bought the extensive wine and grocery business and ran it successfully for 48 years until his death on 10/2/1919 at the age of 63. He was survived by his widow, Elizabeth Galbraith Weir – a daughter of Alexander Weir, Gallowhill Farm – who died in the following year, and by four sons, all of whom left Campbeltown, and two daughters,[112] none of them commemorated on this memorial, a Celtic cross.

22. **McQUEEN**. In this man's life history, which spanned 1839 to 1919, may be discerned some of the elements which made Campbeltown the bustling maritime community it was in the nineteenth century. Archibald McQueen's father, also Archibald, served on the Revenue cutters – based at Campbeltown and operating against smugglers – of which I wrote in the first Kilkerran volume.[113]

Archibald McQueen's father was, in fact, drowned when HM Revenue Cutter *Diligence* was wrecked in a storm, c 1838, off the Giant's Causeway on the north coast of Ireland, with the loss of 46 lives. Archibald Jnr. himself had a spell as a cuttersman, but gave up sailing on ships to learn how to build them. He served his apprenticeship as a carpenter on the Clyde and returned to Campbeltown in the 1860s. He found employment in the boatyard of Duncan McEachran, where the Picture House now stands, and later married his daughter Jean. After Duncan accepted the post of harbourmaster at Campbeltown, Archibald brought into the business another local carpenter, Donald

MacKay, whose gravestone stands nearby.

This association built on an increasingly greater scale, culminating in the ketch *Oimara* and ultimately expanding, with William Broom as a third partner, to become in 1877 the Campbeltown Shipbuilding Company, with its yard at Trench Point, and building not in wood, but in iron. This historic enterprise – from which McQueen withdrew after about seven years – is discussed briefly in Donald MacKay's entry in *An Historical and Genealogical Tour of Kilkerran Graveyard*.[114] McQueen thereafter devoted his energies to public service. In 1868, he was elected to the Town Council, on which he served continuously until his death on 2/3/1919, with a term as Bailie (1890-1908) and as Justice of the Peace for Argyll, among other positions.

Archibald McQueen would unquestionably have been of great assistance in the compilation of this book, and its predecessor, for he had '... a peculiar, even unique knowledge of local affairs, could trace back in memory the history of local families of all classes for generations', and, as Convenor of the Burial Grounds Committee, ' ... his knowledge of lairs and their owners for generations back was remarkable and was frequently of great service, especially to families which had lost touch with the place for lengthened periods'.[115]

The name MacQueen represents *Mac Shuibhne,* from Gaelic *Suibhne* (Sweeney) or Norse *Sveinn*.[116] Despite the relative rarity of the name in Kintyre, Archibald had two other noteworthy namesakes. The Rev John McQueen was born in Lesmahago, Lanarkshire, and was minister of Lochend United Free Church, Campbeltown, between 1883 and 1911. He died at Bearsden in 1916.[117] Donald Macqueen was brought up at Stewarton and for 54 years was employed as a joiner with Argyll Estates. A keen antiquarian, collector of oral tradition, and writer, he died in 1932 at the age of 74.[118]

23. MACNISH/CAMPBELL. MacNish was an unusual name in Kintyre. It derives from Gaelic *Mac Naois*, a shortened form of *Mac Aonghuis*, Son of Angus, and has several anglicised forms, including MacNeish and MacNeice.[119] Neil and John MacNish were tenant-farmers in Margmonach, near Glenbarr, in 1797[120], and in June 1875 Neil McNeish, farmer in Auchencorvie, was seriously injured when run over by a wheel of the cart in which he was transporting peats home from Glecknahavil.[121]

Two brothers Macnish, Neil and Hugh (parents Donald McNish and Mary McMichael) are buried side by side here. Neil, who died on 16/2/1905, aged 68, began his working life as a clerk in Campbeltown and ended up principal partner of Messrs JJ Cochrane & Co, muslin manufacturers of Wellington Mills, Glasgow, and a director of Messrs Stewart, Galbraith & Co, distillers, Campbeltown. He was a 'staunch Conservative', an 'ardent Free Churchman' and a 'most enthusiastic golfer', who captained both Machrihanish and Dunaverty golf clubs.[122] His earlier life was not, however, without tragedy, as the inscription tells: his wife, Agnes Garroway, died in childbirth at the age of 32. He died a very wealthy man, and, since he had no issue, his substantial property holdings in Glasgow were inherited by the four daughters of his brother Hugh.[123]

Hugh – of 'Greenwood Assam', as the inscription records – led a more adventurous life and left many descendants. At about the age of 18, he emigrated to Australia and became a sheep-farmer. 'Away in the wilds of Australia, in the far back bush, he encountered many hardships, and often danger from the aborigines by whom he was surrounded. Sometimes he would speak of the long weary journeys, lasting for months at a time, when sheep were being driven to market, and when the speed was about ten miles per day, and living all the time in the open, on a fare of mutton and damper [flour and water baked in wood ashes.]'

By 1875 he was in India, and in the following year was appointed manager of Greenwood Tea Gardens, where he remained until he retired and returned to Campbeltown in 1895. He was elected to Campbeltown Town Council and served on various of its committees.[124] He died on 8/9/1913 at the age of 72. His first two children, Margaret and Donald, died in infancy and were buried in the cemetery at Dibrugagh, Assam. In 1997, a great-grandson of Hugh's, John C Cunningham, visited the cemetery, but 'the place was in a mess, with lots of people living in [it], and I could find no evidence of their burial'.

Hugh's wife, Grace, survived him by 23 years and died at her house, Lochview, on Kilkerran Road, at the age of 82 on 8/5/1936. She was keen on gardening – one of her pall-bearers was her gardener of more than 25 years, Thomas McCallum – and she was 'never happier than when taking her friends round her garden'. She was survived by four daughters, all of whom married men with high positions in the Colonial administration in India: the eldest, Grace, to Sir Charles Banks Cunningham (no. 2); Florence to Frank W Stewart, District Magistrate at Bellary; Margaret to the Hon Neil McMichael CSI, who was in the Indian judiciary and retired to Campbeltown and lived at Ivybank; Christina to A Ralph Macewen, Secretary to the Board of Revenue, Madras, wounded at Gallipoli in 1915 and subsequently awarded the Military Cross in the Middle East.

Unusually for the time, a Macnish family reunion – after 18 years' separation – was held in the Town Hall, Campbeltown, in 1933, and was attended by more than a hundred family members and friends. During Grace's final illness, three telephone calls from her daughters, Lady Cunningham and Mrs Macewen, reached her from Madras – ' ... the voices in far-away India were heard very distinctly ...' – and were believed to be the first ever telephone communications between India and Campbeltown.

Grace was a daughter of Alexander Campbell (1816-1905), who belonged to a well-established family of tenant-farmers in Southend. His grandparents were Archibald Campbell and Flora McLarty, and his parents Dugald Campbell and Flora McNaughton. In 1846, Alexander married Grace Goold, a daughter of Hugh Goold, the Duke of Argyll's factor in Kintyre. His business ventures ultimately failed, however, and in 1881 he was bankrupted and emigrated to America with his second wife, Elizabeth McNaughton of North Carrine, Southend, whom he had married in 1875. In the Glencoe area of Emmons County, North Dakota, Alexander and his family acquired land and prospered at sheep-farming. He is buried there, but is also commemorated on the stone he raised to his first wife Grace in the old section of Kilkerran.[125]

In 1906, the year after Alexander Campbell's death, his daughter Flora married Angus MacDonald, her long-time fiance.

It seems that Alexander forbade her to marry a MacDonald as long as he remained alive,[126] which goes to show that ancestral prejudice can flourish anew in a foreign climate!

24. **MANSON/WHITEFORD.** In Scotland, the name Manson – derived from Norse *Magnus* – would at once suggest an origin in the Shetlands or a northern part of the mainland, but this Charles Manson in fact came from Denmark, specifically the port of Helsingor, anglicised as Elsinore and the setting of Shakespeare's *Hamlet*. His personal history is something of a puzzle, since he died more than 80 years ago – on 29/12/1925, at the age of 72 – left no memoir and inspired no one to write his obituary (competition, however, was stiff, because Ina MacNeill, Dowager Duchess of Argyll, died just two days later).

Charles had one son, Archie, who married a Campbeltown girl, Janet McGown. They had no sons to continue the Manson name, but the name was perpetuated through connected lines. Captain Charles Mansen (sic) McKinven died in 1976 at the age of 87. Charles 'Charlie' Manson Campbell, fish salesman and ships' chandler in Campbeltown, used his initials CMC for the business which he established in 1980, and one of his twin grandsons, born in 2005, is Jack Manson Campbell. Elizabeth Whiteford, Charles Manson's wife, was Charlie Campbell's great-aunt.

According to family tradition, gathered by Charlie Campbell, Charles Manson arrived in Campbeltown on a grain ship, which he 'jumped'. Certainly, he was already in Campbeltown, aged 25 and married with an infant son, when the 1881 Census was taken. He was variously fisherman, labourer, quay porter and herring-curer, and is remembered for his method of sampling the quality of fish by biting raw specimens.

Elizabeth, his wife (died 3/7/1924, aged 72), was a daughter of John Whiteford and Nancy McMillan, who was born in Southend. Whiteford is a Scottish name – from the lands of Whitefoord, near Paisley[127] – but the Whitefords in Campbeltown migrated here from Ireland.[128] Many of the McKinvens in Campbeltown stem from the marriage of James McKinven,

Charles
Manson
and friend.

53

fisherman, and Mary Whiteford, who married on 12/9/1890, and had eight children: Mary, Janet, Catherine, Donald, James, Jane, Daniel, and Bernard.

25. **THOMSON/MACTAVISH.** Both Hector Thomson and his wife Catherine McArthur belonged to Drumlemble mining families, and would, in an earlier generation, have been buried not in Kilkerran, but in Kilkivan. Golf is the Thomson family's claim to distinction. The first professional appointed to Machrihanish Golf Club was Archie Thomson, in 1920. He was succeeded by his brother Hector, buried here, who died on 5/4/1971 at the age of 93. Remarkably, he was active into his ninetieth year, making him the oldest teaching professional in the world. His son Arthur succeeded him as professional at Machrihanish, retiring in 1986 and dying in 1994. A bricklayer to trade, Arthur was earlier a professional footballer with Clyde FC. Arthur's son, Peter, continues the family tradition into the third generation; he has been professional at Erskine Golf Club since 1978. The brothers Donald and Hugh Thomson from Drumlemble were professionals in Australia in the 1920s.

The best-known golfer to emerge from Kintyre, however, was another Hector Thomson, born in 1913 and a son of Archie, the first professional. He enjoyed a string of successes, including the British Boys' Championship (1931), the Scottish Amateur Championship (1935) and, by a 'spectacular finish', the British Amateur Championship at St Andrews (1936). He played for Scotland in all internationals from 1934 until 1939 and was his country's youngest ever leading player at the age of 21. He twice represented Britain in the Walker Cup and was a member of the team which won the cup for the first time in 1938 at St Andrews. He turned professional in 1940 and maintained his success at that level, winning, among many other honours, the Scottish Professional Championship (1953). In the latter part of his life he was professional at, successively, Milan, Cairo, St Moritz, and Athens, where his father died in 1970 at the age of 89.[129]

The first local DCM of the First World War was a Drumlemble miner, Sergeant Archibald Thomson, who saved the life of a wounded officer at Givenchy, France. Initially in the Argyll and Sutherland Highlanders, he was transferred to the 176th Tunnelling Company of the Royal Engineers.[130]   Sergeant Thomson was accorded an impressive public testimonial in the Argyll Drill Hall in November 1915, but was soon afterwards (2/1/1916) killed by a trench mortar bomb.[131]

The surname Thomson in Kintyre generally represents either Gaelic *Mac Thaimhais* (MacTavish) or *Mac Thomais* (MacComish), eg (from the Old Parish Registers of Campbeltown) Charles Mactavish, woollen carder, and Margaret Morrison, married on 24/9/1827, and Duncan McComish, collier, and Marion McIntosh, married on 2/7/1833.   In the nineteenth century, concentrations of Thomsons were found in and around Skipness and Muasdale as well as Drumlemble.

Incoming Thomsons include an extended family of fishermen from North Berwick who appeared in Campbeltown via Girvan in the 1880s, and Alexander who came to Campbeltown from Buckie in the 1920s to manage the net factory, and whose grandson is Campbeltown-born Professor Joseph McGeachy Thomson (1948-) LLB, FRSE, FRSA, Regius Professor of Law at Glasgow University until his retirement.[132]

This is the type of surname which can mislead genealogists. My wife once assisted a researcher who discovered that her Thomsons abruptly and inexplicably came to an end at a certain point in the trail; but they were there all the time, in their earlier disguise as MacTavishes! The MacTavish name disappeared in Kintyre in the nineteenth century, but continues in Mid Argyll, where, perhaps, the anglicisation trend was less pressing.

The name John McKenzie Mactavish has sunk into obscurity in his native Argyll. A shipwright, he was born into a Tarbert boat-building family on 18/7/1871. In England, in the early part of the twentieth century, he was active as a Socialist and trades unionist, and was General Secretary of the Workers' Educational Association from 1916 to 1927, when retired from his post. He returned to Tarbert in 1936 and died there on 11/7/1938. His published writings comprise 15 brief articles and two pamphlets, *What Labour Wants from Education* (1916) and *Education in its Relation to Labour and Industry* (1919).[133]

Hector Thomson

Another of the name, who merits a mention, is Duncan Campbell Mactavish. He belonged to a fishing family at Castleton, near Lochgilphead, and was Joint County Clerk of Argyll from 1936 until his death on 19/5/1943. He was a contributor to the *Oban Times* and edited *The Gaelic Psalms 1694* (1934). Of greater interest here, however, are his two publications which remain indispensable to genealogists and historians: *The Commons of Argyll*, name-lists of 1685 and 1692, published in 1935, and *Minutes of the Synod of Argyll* in two volumes, 1639-51 and 1652-61, published in 1943 and 1944 for the Scottish History Society. He was a conscientious objector during the First World War and was tried and convicted for his beliefs in 1916, while schoolmaster at Ballachulish.[134]

Division 4

26. McWHIRTER. This family stems from John McWhirter, born in Girvan, Ayrshire, in 1886, and brought up with his mother Catherine Murphy's sister Sabina, who had married Denis McKay, fisherman. The other Murphy sister, Ann, married Denis's brother Archie, also a fisherman, while Catherine herself married yet another Campbeltown fisherman, Duncan McMaster.[135]

John McWhirter, not surprisingly, himself became a fisherman, at the age of 16, after a couple of years in the Post Office, and crewed on the McKay skiffs *Noel* and *Annunciata* until, in 1913, he bought his own skiff, the *Ascension*, from 'Young' John McKay. That same year, on 23 April, he married Rachel Finn, daughter of John Finn and Margaret O'Hara. In 1937, however, he took dermatitis of the hands, which, combined with stomach trouble, decided him to come ashore. Rachel died on 23/1/1968, aged 79, and John on 26/8/1979, aged 92. During 1974-76, I tape-recorded many hours of interviews with John, and preserved from his remarkable memory a fund of information and stories which furnished material for four books ... five, if this one may be included!

His second-born son, Seaman Thomas Finn McWhirter, died on 15/4/1943, aged 27, while serving on *HMT Adonis*. He was acting as a 'spotter', during enemy action, when his vessel was torpedoed, and he was last seen swimming strongly and assisting a shipmate who was a non-swimmer. 'Those who knew "Tommy", as he was affectionately known, will not be surprised that he lost his life in trying to save one of his shipmates.' His body was recovered days later, by chance, and returned to Campbeltown for burial. He had intended to marry on his next leave and during his final leave had made arrangements for the wedding.[136] His fiancee was Margaret McAdam, from the Dumbarton area, and she was a WREN – a member of the Women's Royal Navy Service – stationed in Campbeltown. After Tommy's death, she corresponded with his mother for many years, but the family later lost touch with her.[137]

When Thomas left school he was apprenticed as a baker with JC McMurchy, then became a fisherman and finally worked with Cefoil Ltd., which operated the pioneering seaweed-processing factory near Bellochantuy, 1935-42. Like his father, and others of the McWhirter family, he was a talented footballer and played locally with Campbeltown Grammar School Former Pupils FC.[138]

The name McWhirter originated in Ayrshire and represents Gaelic *Mac Chruiteir*, son of the harpist or fiddler.[139]

27. **HUNTER.** This grave holds a solitary occupant whose death came suddenly in a small theatre of war. Thomas Hunter, adviser for the West of Scotland Agricultural College in south Argyll, was one of two fatalities – the other was a local lorry-driver, Alexander Blue – in the first of the two German air-raids on Campbeltown, on 6 November, 1940. Thomas, aged 51, died the following day in the Cottage Hospital.[140]

Owing to wartime censorship, the raid passed unreported in the *Campbeltown Courier*; likewise in Thomas Hunter's local newspaper, the *Galloway Gazette*, which published the following sparse, but poignant obituary.

The death has occurred of Mr Thomas Hunter, an organiser of the West of Scotland Agricultural College for the past 18 years.

Thomas
Hunter

Campbeltown War
Memorial.

Deceased, who was well known in the Stewartry, was a son of the late Mr Thomas Hunter, The Mark, Creetown, and was a brother of Mrs Gardiner, wife of Mr John Gardiner, Upper Rosco, Gatehouse, a member of the Stewartry County Council.

A well known figure in the Northern Islands, Mr Hunter was intimately associated with the introduction of the Paris Green Bran insecticide which proved such a boon to farmers in the treatment of land which was likely to be grubbed in oats.

A Bulletin was issued by the West of Scotland College based upon the results of his investigations and organising research.

An excellent golfer, he took part in many club and county competitions, while he prominently identified himself with the task of supervising extensive green improvements at a well known golf course on the West coast.[141]

That three English sailors attached to HMS *Nimrod* were also killed during that raid is one of the little-known facts of the local war record. Ordinary Seamen Richard Howard Cookson, Harry Fitton and Michael Holmes, all from Lancashire, were together outside the Victoria Hall when a 500lb serial bomb was dropped close beside them from a low altitude.[142] Michael Holmes was buried at Liverpool (Ford) Cemetery and the others at sea.

28. **SYDENHAM, TAYLOR**. There is a scattering of military gravestones throughout the cemetery, but by far the greatest concentration lines a pathway on the higher ground, immediately below the imposing white memorial cross. These fatalities belong to the Second World War, when south Kintyre was a hive of naval activity, with HMS *Nimrod* in Campbeltown and HMS *Landrail* at Machrihanish airfield. Some of them died unspectacularly, the victims of routine training accidents, while others perished in events which take us a little closer to the hub of the war.

One of the greatest disasters represented here – by one of her crew and a passenger – was the crash of a Liberator aircraft on 1 September 1941, near the head of Balnabraid Glen. Although designed as a bomber, the Liberator's long range made it one of the most versatile aircraft of the Second World War. Suitably modified and equipped, it played an important role in U-boat detection and destruction in the Battle of the Atlantic. A further key role was as a transport plane, modified to provide fuel capacity allowing non-stop flights of over 3,100 miles.[143]

Liberator AM915, which crashed on Kintyre, was such a transport plane, engaged in the BOAC Return Ferry Service, which began operations over the North Atlantic on 4 May 1941. The original purpose was to return to Canada air crews which had delivered American-built aircraft to the UK, but the service was increasingly used by VIPs and technical experts valuable to the British war effort.

Indeed, on board AM915, in addition to her crew of four, were six passengers, including a Belgian, Count Guy de Baillet-Latour, who seems certain to have been involved in an earlier shipment to the United States of 1,250 tons of uranium oxide ore, which was stored in 2000 steel drums at Port Richmond, Staten Island, and which theoretically contained sufficient uranium for the manufacture of the three atomic bombs exploded in 1945. That there was an unrecovered phial of radium aboard Liberator AM915 is confirmed in the official accident report precis. Local tradition had it that a special constable, who was at the scene of the crash, appropriated it without realising what it was.

The cause of the crash remains uncertain, but recent research by Mr Ian Davies, an aviation historian, points to a failure in radio communications. What is certain is that Liberator AM915 flew from Montreal on 31 August at 1319 Greenwich Mean Time, arrived for refuelling at RCAF Gander, Newfoundland, at 1805, and left there at 2226, with an estimated arrival at RAF Heathfield, Ayr, of 0759, 1 September. When she arrived over Ayrshire at 0800, the cloud base was 2000 ft. and visibility 12 miles. Using standard bad weather procedure, she could have landed at Ayr in these conditions, but Captain Kenneth Garden

S.W. Sydenham

LIBERATOR
IN HANGAR.

decided to divert to Squires Gate, Blackpool, which, however, was already closing owing to bad weather. Unable to land there, he decided to return to Ayr, heading on a navigational track which took him towards Kintyre. Shortly after 0936, radio communication was lost, AM915 failed to make the turn towards Ayr at the appropriate time, and a few minutes later, at 1010, crashed.

All 10 persons aboard were killed. Four crew: Captain KD Garden (Australian); First Officer GL Panes (British), both of British Airways, but seconded to the Ministry of Aircraft Production for Atlantic ferrying duties; Radio Officer SW Sydenham (Canadian); Flight Engineer CA Spence (American). Civilians: RB Mowat, Professor of History at Bristol University, who had been lecturing in the US for the Carnegie Trust; Count Baillet-Latour, Economic Counsellor in London to the Belgian Ministry of Colonies; Dr M Benjamin of the Central Scientific Office in Washington (British); Captain S Picking, US Navy; Mr BY Taylor of Farnborough (British), and Lieut Col LH Wrangham, Royal Marines (British).

Calum Bannatyne, then shepherd at Auchenhoan, was alerted to the crash by an airborne trail of charred paper, which he noticed while working at the Auchenhoan sheep-fanks. The crash is commemorated by a marker within the forest on Arinarach Hill at NR 734 156, and, though the wreckage was cleared, metal fragments may still be encountered on the slopes of Balnabraid Glen.[144]

Three weeks earlier, on 10 August, Liberator AM261 had crashed on Am Binnein, Arran, with the loss of 21 lives, mostly ferry pilots returning to Canada to bring more aircraft across the Atlantic. She had taken off, in bad weather, from RAF Heathfield, Ayr, for Gander, Newfoundland, on a true track of 293 degrees instead of 273 degrees, and 10 minutes later crashed at 2,650 ft. when she should have cleared Arran at about 4,000 ft. The accident was attributed to unknown navigational errors. Lord Beaverbrook was scheduled to cross the Atlantic on that flight, but switched on the day to Liberator AM915, the one which later crashed in Kintyre.

From the two Kintyre Liberator graves, the Arran mountains can be seen in the north-east, beyond Davaar Island. In the east can be seen the coast of Ayrshire, where a third Liberator, AM260, crashed four days after the Arran one, while taking off from RAF Heathfield. All in all, a nasty spell for the BOAC Return Ferry Service, and all the more remarkable for the fact that no other ferry casualties occurred on this side of the Atlantic throughout the entire war.[145]

Division 3

29. **MACDONALD.** Despite Kintyre's long association with Clan Donald, the surname MacDonald has never been a common one here. It is certain that most of the MacDonald families at present in Campbeltown came originally from various parts of the Highlands and Islands during the nineteenth and twentieth centuries. Andrew McKerral has explained that absence succinctly as it relates to Kintyre: 'Apart from the leading families of Dunnyveg, Largie, and Sanda, this name was not borne by any occupier of land in the sixteenth-century lists. The lists of 1596 and 1605 contain a few of the name, but they are easily identifiable as belonging to one or other of the three above families.'[146] The history of that most powerful of medieval Gaelic clans has been extensively documented, and it will suffice to state here that the surname derives from Donald of Islay, son of Ranald and grandson of Somerled, who was assassinated in 1164 at Renfrew while leading an expedition against King Malcolm IV of Scotland.

Thomas MacDonald, who is buried here, belonged to a family which originated in Inverness-shire. His shepherd grandfather, Angus MacDonald, was born in October 1840 in the Parish of Kilmonivaig, bordering on Perthshire, to Donald MacDonald and Flora Kennedy. His first wife, Annie MacRae, died at Largie. His second wife was Janet Watson, who was born at Lochend, Campbeltown, and died in 1895. Angus himself

64

Thomas MacDonald

died at Killeonan in 1904. From the birthplaces of his three children, his movement south into Kintyre can be roughly plotted. Alexander was born in Gairloch, Wester Ross, Donald in Glenballoch, Arrochar, and Annie – by his second marriage – in Crossibeg.[147]

Thomas was a son of Alexander MacDonald and Frances Kelly (born in South Uist). A 'boy messenger' in the Post Office, he was accidentally shot dead on 4 December 1943, after delivering telegrams to Stronvaar House, which was then in the possession of the Navy. Thomas was 16 years old, and the sentry who shot him – Denis Kavanagh of Cleator Moor, Cumberland – was himself just 19.

Susan Robertson, who was a near-neighbour of Tommy's in Park Square, told the fatal accident enquiry in February that she had met him 'on the pier' and that the two of them walked off together, he to deliver telegrams and she to deliver newspapers. At Stronvaar, Tommy stopped to talk to the sentry while she went into the house with the papers; and the two were again talking together – Tommy's telegrams by then delivered – when she left them and went on her way. Then she heard a shot. 'Tommy was lying beside a hedge and the sentry was bending over him. The sentry seemed worried and asked me to get a doctor. I went into Stronvaar to do what I could.'

Tommy was killed by a single bullet in the chest. A gunnery officer, Lieut. George Donald Banks, had examined the rifle two days after the fatal shooting and testified before the enquiry that the safety catch was functioning properly and that all other parts of the rifle were in working order.

Ordinary Seaman Kavanagh denied responsibility. 'I knew Thomas MacDonald and was on friendly terms with him. He came up that evening while I was on duty and I had a word with him. We were teasing one another in a friendly manner. While we were still talking my rifle went off and he collapsed. I bent over him and sent for help right away. I did not point the rifle at him. I pulled the bolt back and the rifle went off. I am positive I never touched the trigger.'

In the judgement of Sheriff KA Borland, the shooting was accidental, but Thomas's father Alexander, described as a retired ploughman, later pursued Denis Kavanagh for damages on the grounds that he had 'suffered severely in his feelings, and he has also suffered pecuniary loss'. Aside from his late son's wage of £1 1s, Alexander MacDonald had had no income but his old age pension of 10s and the 7s 'allotment' received weekly from his other son, who was serving in the Navy. He had originally sought £1000, but settled for £435.[148]

30. **COLVILLE**. GF Black ascribes to this name a Norman origin – Coleville, ie Col's vill or farm, probably the town between Caen and Bayeux – and records the first of the name in Scotland as Philip de Coleuille, *circa* 1159.[149] That origin, however, hardly entitles every Colville family to assume Norman descent. Outwith the ranks of the wealthy and powerful, hereditary surnames developed slowly. Many among the commonalty of the late Middle Ages would adopt the surname of their feudal superior or clan chief, and in the transfer of loyalty from one family to another, whether by choice or under duress, one name could be discarded and another taken just a simply as the changing of a suit of clothes.

 In a memoir of the Campbeltown-born evangelist, John Colville (1827-96), by his widow, Mary Agnes Bodington, an account of the Colvilles' appearance in Kintyre includes the claim that streams of refugees from persecution came to Kintyre not only from 'different parts of Scotland', but 'also from some parts of the Continent', in the sixteenth as well as the seventeenth century.[150] This, as history, is absurd, but its author may be forgiven, since there were few reliable historical sources to consult at the time she wrote. In fact, the Colvilles came to Kintyre in the mid-seventeenth century as part of a politically and militarily motivated settlement, encouraged by the Campbell Marquess of Argyll and pioneered by such Lowland lairds as William Ralston of that Ilk, who had estates in Beith and Lochwinnoch.

 The occupant of this grave, Duncan Colville, is unlikely to have entertained any illusions concerning his ancestry, genealogy having been one of his many interests. The facts are that the first known Colvilles in Kintyre were recorded in the farm of

Gartgreillan, Glen Lussa, during the decade 1663-1673: John and his wife Betty Armour, William and Jenat Anderson, and Robert and Elizabeth Cathcart. An origin in the locality of West Kilbride, Ayrshire, was postulated by Duncan Colville, albeit on the basis of incomplete evidence; but, wherever they came from, all the Colville families in Kintyre, with one (recent) exception, are believed to descend from these three families.[151]

Duncan Colville was born into a Campbeltown whisky family in 1883 – his father was David Colville of The Hall, Dalintober – and as his obituarist in the *Kintyre Magazine* explained: 'He lived in circumstances which permitted him the means and the time to follow his own inclinations, and he belonged to a generation which often used its leisure in an erudite and constructive way.'[152] That was certainly true of Duncan Colville, whose gargantuan research labours turned him into a local authority on an impressive range of subjects – archaeology, genealogy, history, natural history, and place-names, to list the main ones – some of which, at the time, were effectively the preserve of professionals. His pioneering studies in the prehistory and history of Kintyre constitute a legacy of inestimable value; inestimable because, regrettably, he was not a prolific writer, and his extensive collection of manuscripts and notebooks has been dispersed. Yet, he was a writer of real ability, as proof of which see his absorbing 'Survey of the Place Names of the Burgh of Campbeltown', serialised in the *Campbeltown Courier* from 3 April to 29 May, 1937. His 'Notes on the Standing Stones of Kintyre'[153] won the prestigious Chalmers-Jarvise Prize Essay in 1929. His writings – published and unpublished – remain to be collected.

Duncan was educated in Edinburgh and lived there for a time, but he spent most of his long life – he was almost 98 years old when he died on 1/5/1981 – in Campbeltown. He was a founder-member of the Kintyre Antiquarian Society in 1921, its first Secretary (1921-25), its President (1947-66), and, finally, its Honorary President.[154] He was a Justice of the Peace and Director of Campbeltown Savings Bank, among other offices. His outdoor pursuits included shooting, fishing and golfing. In 1971, along with his fellow-antiquarian and friend, Fr James Webb (1883-1975), he was given the highest honour which the Royal Burgh of Campbeltown could bestow, that of Freeman. At the time of their presentation, he and Fr Webb had amassed between them 177 years. Rory Colville, born in 1947 and an Argyll and Bute Councillor for Kintyre, is a grandson of Duncan Colville.

Like many other families of Lowland Plantation stock in Kintyre, the Colvilles/Colvills prospered, not least in the booming whisky-distilling industry of the nineteenth century, and among those who left Kintyre to find prosperity in the industrial Lowlands were David Colville (1813-98), iron and steel master, and John Colville (1844-1924) of the Glasgow Cotton Spinning Co Ltd.[155]

Not all Kintyre Colvilles, however, prospered. The Campbeltown Registers of Poor contain the names of some whose lives were tied to humbler destinies, such as Elizabeth McNeill of Gigha, whose husband, John Colville, a joiner, was killed in America, in 1882, 18 months after the family had emigrated, necessitating her and her children's return to Campbeltown, their voyage paid by the Caledonian Club, and 4s a week poor relief at the end of it[156]; or John Colville, Lochend, a distillery worker who injured his leg in 1866 and received 5s a week to keep him, his wife Agnes McAlister and their four youngest children.[157] The name Colville remains strongly represented in south Kintyre – all 19 Colvilles listed in the Lomond and Argyll telephone directory for 2009/10 share the code 01586.

Duncan Colville's wife, Mary Fleming Gilchrist, died in the Cottage Hospital, Campbeltown, on 23/7/1940, having suffered a blood-clot during a minor operation. She was 49 years old; he thus almost doubled her lifespan in his own. She was a daughter of Alexander Gilchrist, Ballevain, and Mary Fleming, who died on Christmas Day 1890 at the age of 26, five days after giving birth to her.

The name Gilchrist – from Gaelic *Mac Gille Criosd*, 'Son of the Servant of Christ' – is not included in Andrew McKerral's appendix of 'Highland Personal Names' in *Kintyre in the Seventeenth Century*, but is on record in Kintyre towards the end of that century – Murdoch McGilchrist in Tangitavill and Lagalgarv and John McGilchrist in Killarow in 1694[158] – and by 1797 six names appear in the Work Horse Tax list for Kintyre, all as 'Gilchrist': Neil in Gartincopaig, Angus and Malcom in Margad (near Clachan), Duncan in Dumnaleck (also near Clachan), Peter in Carnmore and William in Corputechan.[159] By the end of the nineteenth century, Gilchrist families were well represented and widely intermarried in the Campbeltown fishing community.

31. **MARTIN**. Neil McInnes Martin, interred here with his second wife, was my grandfather's brother. He was born on 12/7/1881 in Queen Street, Dalintober. His paternal parents and grandparents are interred in Kilchousland, the traditional burial ground of the Dalintober folk until the little churchyard filled up. Neil 'Hairy' was unquestionably a 'character', a status measurable by the number of associated anecdotes – the more stories, the greater the character. It's no science, but the principle works well enough across two or three generations, after which the character, having dropped out of living memory, begins to drop out of oral tradition too, unless held there by truly heroic or infamous exploits.

My father's cousin, Willie Martin, maintained that 'a childhood prank spoiled Neil's character'.[160] Willie did not elaborate, and I might never have known what the incident was had it not been reported in the local newspapers. In April 1894, Neil, who was 14, and a younger companion, Duncan Graham, made two appearances in the Burgh Police Court. In the first case, they pled guilty to having 'placed a line or cord across High Askomil Road, to the danger of passengers'. The device succeeded on the night of 2 April and a domestic servant was tripped and fell. The police constable 'reported Martin to be a very bad boy, continually giving the police annoyance', and also that when he called on Martin's father 'he got nothing but the height of impudence'. The boys were dismissed, having been severely reprimanded and threatened with a birching if they reappeared before the court. On a charge of stealing four eggs from a henhouse in the garden of Braefoot, High Street, Neil was fined 5s and Duncan 2s 6d, with the alternative of 48 hours' imprisonment. Duncan's 'paternal relative' was reported as being present in court, but 'Martin's parents refused to have anything to do with him'.[161]

These highly embarrassing reports elicited from Neil's father, John Martin – a successful fisherman and a property-owner – an immediate response, which appeared as a letter, headed 'A PROTEST', in the following week's issue of the *Campbeltown Courier*. To the allegation that he 'refused to have anything to do with him', John stated that he 'knew nothing of the case whatever till after it was all over'. He also denied that he had been visited by the police constable, let alone given him 'the height of impudence'. 'Allow me, Sir,' he concluded, 'to protest against such misstatements being made in Court without due enquiry, and also, as a parent, against lads of 14 and 11 years of age being arrested and tried as criminals without notice being given to their natural guardians to attend and see that they obtain fair play.'

That Neil became the 'black sheep' of the family is a certainty, but whether these juvenile transgressions – trivial by modern standards – were influential factors, I leave to the judgement of psychologists. In truth, drink was Neil's folly, and as the only brother of ten who gave himself to the bottle, his folly seems the more pronounced. Tales of his exploits abound: a confrontation with Sheriff John Macmaster Campbell CBE – Lochaber-born historian and Gaelic activist – during which he threatened to shoot Campbell's dog, which had menaced him; the theft of an ice-cream barrow found unattended outside an Ayr cafe, and the reckless distribution of free 'pokey hats' to the children of the town; his comical, drunken fights with his cousin Donald 'Ban' Martin, which invariably ended with Neil's arm going out of joint and having to be helped back into place by his adversary. Yet, for all his failings, Neil was popular, not least among children.

Later in life, Neil abandoned his wild ways and became religious, a transformation attributed to his having fallen while felling trees for net-poles. This accident, which happened in 1933, was reported in the *Campbeltown Courier* under the headline, 'FISHERMAN'S MIRACULOUS ESCAPE FROM DEATH'. He had gone alone to Saddell and was 'standing on one of the topmost branches of a fir, using a hatchet to lop off some of the higher foliage', when he lost his balance and plummeted 30 feet to the ground. Fortunately for him, two Saddell workmen happened to be nearby and immediately telephoned for the town ambulance, which rushed him to the Cottage Hospital. He remained 'quite conscious' throughout his ordeal, and x-rays revealed 'severe injuries to the spine'[162] Apparently, and understandably, he had feared for his life; but he recovered, gave up alcohol, 'could quote the Bible from back to front' and took to playing hymns on his piano.

Neil was unfortunate in marriage. His first wife, Christina Wylie, whom he married in 1910, died of peritonitis, at the age of 23, less than two years later. Their sons were brought up apart, Tommy with the Wylie family and Johnny with Neil's unmarried sister, Sarah, until Neil remarried and Johnny returned to his father. Neil's second wife was Flora Currie, whom Willie Martin described as a 'lovely lady'; but he felt that the relationship lacked 'passion' and that Neil never recovered from the death of Christina.[163] He first skippered the little family skiff *Bella*, then, in 1913, had a new skiff, the *Amethyst*, built at McMillan's boatyard, Tarbert. His last boat was the *Renown* and he died at the age of 74 on 18/2/1955.

Tommy Martin was tried in 1935 on charges of reckless driving and culpable homicide 'while under the influence of intoxicating liquor'. The jury found the reckless driving charge not proven and Martin not guilty on the culpable homicide charge. On 29 December 1934, near Tayinloan, Martin's car had struck a motor cyclist, Duncan McCallum, who died along with his passenger, William Hawthorn.[164]

There are, in Campbeltown, several Martin families which can be traced back to the eighteenth century in Kintyre and some of which may be interconnected.

My own family is traceable only as far back as Duncan Martin and Mary McCallum, who lived at Achnasavil, Carradale, in the

Neil Martin

1780s, and then at Torrisdale, before a part of the family moved to Dalintober in the first quarter of the nineteenth century and joined the expanding fishing community there. The 'Dalintober Martins' also include the fishing family to which belonged the notable Captain Duncan Martin (1855-1915), whose daughter Katherine in 1901 founded the bookshop at 14 Main Street, which is still known as 'Martin's' and still family-owned. Typical forenames were Angus, Duncan and John.

In Campbeltown itself, there was another Martin fishing family – principal member Robert 'Brannan' Martin (died 1911, aged 54) – which can be traced back to John Martin, seaman, and Mary Smith, who were married in 1797 in Killean and Kilchenzie Parish. Typical names in this family were Charles, Robert and John.

The Martin family of joiners in Campbeltown also originated in Killean and Kilchenzie Parish and stemmed from Donald Martin – son of Charles Martin, farmer, and Janet Gilchrist – who was a maltster in Campbeltown and died on 2/9/1888 at the age of 75. His wife Agnes was a daughter of John McQuistan and Mary Milloy and died on 20/9/1891 at the age of 79. Typical names in this family are Donald and Malcolm.

An extensive family of Martins stemmed from the marriage of James Martin and Mary McArthur on 7/1/1890. His parents were John Martin, mason, and Mary Killen (married on 30/4/1866) and his grandparents Malcolm Martin, mason, and Mary McKillop. Typical names in this family: Charles, James and John.

Other Martin families in Campbeltown may or may not be connected with the above. The genealogies present a complex entanglement which I have not yet been able to unravel. The form of the name in the earliest tenantry records of Kintyre is generally 'McIlmartin', which represents Gaelic *Mac Gille Mhartain*, 'Son of the Servant of [Saint] Martin'.

Appendices and Addenda

1. The Dugald Haston Connection.

Mrs Maria McSporran McIntyre, Campbeltown, has explained the precise connection of mountaineer Dugald Haston with Campbeltown, referred to on p 48 of *An Historical and Genealogical Tour of Kilkerran Graveyard*. He was a son of Margaret Curdie McSporran, born 6/2/1900, in Longrow, Campbeltown, who married Robert Bremner Haston, baker, on 10/10/1927 at Lasswade, Midlothian. Dugald's maternal grandparents were Duncan Curdie McSporran and Penelope Mitchell (married 26/11/1897, Killean Parish) and his great-grandparents Archibald McSporran, distillery workman, and Maria Curdie, and John Mitchell, gamekeeper, and Marion McMillan. The Curdie line in Kintyre can be taken back to Charles Curdie, quarrier, and Margaret McMath.

2. Flory Loynachan: Person, Poem and Putative Authors.

Flory Loynachan was a real person, born on 13/3/1810 to John Loynachan of Shennachie on the southern Learside, and Florence McEachran, who married in 1808. Archie McEachran, Kilblaan, records that Flory – 'a wee round-faced girl' – went to Kilblaan in 1832 to 'keep house' after the death of his great-grandmother, and that the poem was composed, during her service there, 'by one who seems to have loved her deeply'. Flory later emigrated to Ontario, Canada.[165]

The poem may or may not be a genuine expression of love. It is certainly a seriously dense assemblage of local dialect words, which probably explains why it has failed to travel well and has remained in the repertoire of local singers. In recent years, the song was revived by John Morris, Glasgow, who first heard it sung by an aunt, Ellen Lang McSporran, who herself heard it from Willie Colville, both latterly of Machrihanish. John himself descends on his maternal line from Edward Lang, seaman, Dalintober, and Agnes Milloy, who married on 23/12/1856.

Edward's parents were Neil Lang, mason, and Barbara Milloy, and Agnes's were John Milloy, shepherd, Knockscalbert, and Isabella McIntyre. Local singer, Anne Leith, who performs with the group Wild Sarachs, has since bravely added 'Flory Loynachan' to her repertoire.

Archie McEachran credited the poem's composition to a Campbeltown fisherman, John McLean, who died in the cholera epidemic of 1854 and is buried in a field on Arran,[166] but also recognised the claim of Dugald MacIlreavie, Corbett's Close, whose sung version was published, with glossary, in the *Campbeltown Courier* of 2/5/1903 – its second appearance – then reproduced, without the glossary, as a postcard by K & J Martin, 14 Main Street. MacIlreavie was again credited with its composition in the introductory notes to a slightly different version published in 1927 in the 'Kintyriana' series in the *Campbeltown Courier*,[167] that being the version which Latimer McInnes quoted in his *Dialect of South Kintyre* of 1934. To the names John McLean and Dugald Macilreavie may be added that of George Stewart – an employee of the Clyde Trust and 'pioneer of amateur photography'[168] – and the Rev Neil Brodie[169]. Given the technical polish of the composition, Neil Brodie's may be the greatest claim. Further, since Loynachan and Brolachan were the two outstanding 'O' names of the nineteenth century, their conjunction in the solution of this literary puzzle would be fitting; but the truth will almost certainly never be known.

Surnames prefixed by 'O' – descendant of – were once common in Kintyre and presumably reflect the geographical proximity of Kintyre to thè north of Ireland, and the strong cultural and genealogical links between these two Gaelic-speaking areas. The name Loynachan had effectively disappeared from Kintyre – indeed from Scotland – by the end of the nineteenth century. It was therefore a surprise when Mr Jerry Loynachan arrived in Kintyre with his daughter Laura in April 2009, from Arizona, USA, to research his family's origins. The old form of the name is alive and well in North America![170]

3. Proudfoot McIntyre.

Discussing this unusual name on p 64 of *An Historical and Genealogical Tour of Kilkerran Graveyard*, I speculated that it might derive from an Inland Revenue officer, Patrick MacFarlane Proudfoot. Mrs Margaret Thomson – nee McIntyre – has written from Lochgilphead (16/5/2007) to say that Proudfoot 'was called for his Great Grandmother Janet (Jessie) Proudfoot who married Thomas Merrylees on 21st June 1844 at Skirling, Peebles'. Proudfoot Hannah McIntyre, she adds, was born on 19/8/1895, and brought up by his grandparents, Alexander McIntyre and Margaret Merrilees. He died of heart failure at Hillside Farm on 6/5/1921 and is listed on Campbeltown War Memorial as a casualty of the First World War.

4. Macmillan Family.

Mrs Barbara Wilkie points out a mistake in the family tree of Daniel McMillan on p 24 of *An Historical and Genealogical Tour of Kilkerran Graveyard*. His grandfather was William Macmillan, 'who farmed Kilmichael after Daniel or Donald, and Isabella Porter, his parents. William gave up the lease and became a distillery maltman'. John Macmillan, Coledrain, who married Anne Langwill, was William's brother and from him Mrs Wilkie's line of Macmillans stems.

5. Jessie Eliza Weir.

This daughter of the Rev Walter Weir – *An Historical and Genealogical Tour of Kilkerran Graveyard*, pp. 21-22 – is stated to have married a Samuel Greenlees. He was, in fact, the Kintyre-born pioneering whisky-blender of the firm Greenlees Brothers, and he and Jessie Eliza are buried in Kilkerran (western wall, Division 3) under a monument of imposing proportions. See *Kintyre Magazine* No. 67, pp. 13-18.

6. Dr. Campbell MacKinnon MD CB

Mr John C Cunningham, Honiton, Devon, informs me that a detailed service record of   Dr Campbell MacKinnon MD CB – No. 12 in *An Historical and Genealogical Tour of Kilkerran*

Graveyard – can be sourced in DG Crawford's *Roll of the Indian Medical Service, 1615-1930*, London 1930, p 101. John Campbell MacKinnon, who died in 1906 and is buried in Fulham, London, is commemorated alongside his father's memorial on a small stone propped against the wall.

References and Notes

In these references and notes, *Argyllshire Herald* is abbreviated to *AH*, *Campbeltown Courier* to CC, *The Kintyre Magazine* to *KM*, and Registers of Poor, Campbeltown Parish, to RP.

1. A Martin, *Kintyre Country Life*, Edinburgh 1987, pp. 188-89.
2. A Martin, *An Historical and Genealogical Tour of Kilkerran Graveyard*, Campbeltown 2006, pp. 9-10.
3. CC, 11/12/1875.
4. *AH*, 8/12/1866.
5. Minute Book, Parochial Board of Campbeltown, 8/1/1867, CO 6/7/4/3, Argyll & Bute Archive, Lochgilphead.
6. CC, 11/1/1908.
7. *The Oxford Names Companion*, Oxford 2002, p 153.
8. CC, 28/12/1918.
9. JC Cunningham, letter, 31/10/2006.
10. *AH*, 3/11/1917.
11. *The Times*, obit, 31/10/1967.
12. JC Cunningham, *op. cit.*
13. Kintyre Antiquarian Society report, undated; JC Cunningham, *Ibid.*
14. JC Cunningham, *Ibid.*
15. A McKerral, *Kintyre in the Seventeenth Century*, Edinburgh 1948, p 82.
16. *Ibid.*
17. *KM* No. 56, p 22.
18. *CC*, obit 31/1/1925.
19. *Ibid*, 17/7/1911.
20. A McKinven, *KM* No. 49, p 8.
21. CC, 15/8/1936.
22. A Orde Hume, *British Commercial Aeroplanes 1920-1940 in Detail*, 2003, p 454.
23. CC, 15/8/1936.
24. *Ibid*, 22/8/1936.

25. J Arbuckle, letter 18/10/2006.
26. *Ibid*, letter 19/10/2006.
27. *AH*, 16/1/1869.
28. J Currie, *Mull Family Names*, Mull 1998, p 55, and File of Mull Inhabitants, Currie Collection, Mull Museum.
29. *The Oxford Names Companion, op. cit.*, p 421.
30. Alastair Campbell of Airds, letter 24/10/2006.
31. *CC*, 17/11/1917, DSO award & 7/3/1942, obit; Mactaggart family papers, courtesy of John Mactaggart, Campbeltown.
32. *AH*, obit 7/8/1875.
33. DC Mactavish, *The Commons of Argyll*, Lochgilphead 1935, p 2.
34. K Veitch, The European Ethnological Research Centre, letter 23/11/2006.
35. 'The McKersie Family in Kintyre', genealogical notes by Mr William Norman McKersie, Pinner, 2/11/2006; *CC*, 12/11/1904, obit Ex-Provost John McKersie; gravestone inscriptions, Kilkerran.
36. *Fasti Ecclesiae Scoticanae,* Vol 3, Synod of Glasgow & Ayr, Edinburgh 1920, p 111.
37. OPR. Neill Brolachan, born 19/2/ and baptised 22/2/1813.
38. *Collins Encyclopaedia of Scotland*, eds. John & Julia Keay, London 1992, p 668.
39. *Ibid.*, p 230.
40. *Fasti Ecclesiae Scoticanae, op. cit.*
41. *AH*, 19/3/1892.
42. *Ibid.*, 8/11/1861.
43. Edinburgh 1984, p 42.
44. GF Black, *The Surnames of Scotland,* original edition New York 1946, reissued Edinburgh 1993, p 104.
45. AJ MacVicar, *The Book of Blaan*, Oban 1965, p 60.
46. Letters, 23/3/1983 & 25/3/1983.
47. *Op. cit.*, p 208.
48. *AH*, 24/11/1866.
49. A Martin, *Kintyre: The Hidden Past*, Edinburgh 1984, pp. 200 & 209.
50. R Bell, *Ulster Surnames*, Belfast 1988, pp. 20-21.

51. M Heggen, 'The Holmes Family of Campbeltown', KM No. 59, p 4.
52. Information from Ms Jane Reid, Campbeltown, 12 and 22/5/2007.
53. *CC* & *AH*, 15/2/1913.
54. Mr Webb Clark, McPherson, Kansas, USA, letter 16/3/1992.
55. *CC* & *AH*, 6/11/1909;
http://www.gnb.ca/cnb/grand/ship-e.asp
56. *The Oxford Names Companion*, op. cit., pp. 259 & 260; GF Black, *op. cit.*, p 323.
57. A Martin, *An Historical and Genealogical Tour ... Campbeltown 2006*, pp. 11-13.
58. Ed AIB Stewart, *List of the Inhabitants upon the Duke of Argyle's Property in Kintyre in 1792*, Edinburgh 1991, p 219.
59. R Bell, op. cit., p 80.
60. A Martin, *The Ring-Net Fishermen*, Edinburgh 1981, pp. 4-25.
61. *AH*, 18/4/1862.
62. A Martin, *Kintyre: The Hidden Past*, *op. cit*, pp. 203 and 205; *AH*, 3/1/1862. The former source states 'West Indies', and the latter – which may be preferred for accuracy – 'East Indies'.
63. *AH*, 3/1/1862.
64. *Ibid*, 17/1/1862.
65. RP 707.
66. R Bell, *op. cit.*, p 209.
67. GF Black, *op. cit.*, p 550; *The Oxford Names Companion*, *op. cit.*, p 421, under McNelis.
68. DC MacTavish, *op. cit.*, pp. 47 & 48.
69. Hearth Tax List, Scottish Record Office, E69/3, pp. 51 and 52.
70. Ed AIB Stewart, *op.* cit., pp. 277-8.
71. OPR, Campbeltown.
72. E Gauldie, *KM* No. 51, pp. 18-20.
73. *CC*, 6/6/ & 11/7/1903.
74. *CC*, 28/10/1922.

75. A Martin, *An Historical and Genealogical Tour ...,*   *op. cit.*, p 49.
76. CC, 9/3/1918.
77. CC, 22/4/1954.
78. Aberdeen 1995, pp. 49-50.
79. *CC, op. cit.*
80. M Speed, letter, 4/11/2006.
81. http://www.watersideweb.co.uk
82. http://www.historic-uk.com
83. *CC,* 20/12/1941 & 20/2/1943.
84. Family documents and personal memories from Mrs Norma McDougall, 22/10/2006.
85. RP 931.
86. *Ibid.* 1965.
87. Personal documents and memories; the researches of Candy Crawford Rae; documents held by Mrs May Barbour, Southend, daughter of the late Archibald MacKay, Lephenstrath; *KM* No. 40, pp. 27-29; *Herald,* 5/12/2001, obit of Prof Iain Boyle.
88. *The Oxford Names Companion, op. cit.*, p 342, under 'Kilbride'.
89. GF Black, *op. cit.* p 460.
90. Duncan C Mactavish, *op. cit.* p 48.
91. Work Horse Tax, *op. cit.*
92. *AH,* 3/10/1862.
93. *CC,* 29/2/1896, 8/2/1908 & 28/8/1909.
94. *CC,* 4/5 & 27/6/1912.
95. Register of Deaths, Campbeltown, 25/8/1909.
96. A Martin, *Fish and Fisherfolk*, Colonsay 2004, p 165.
97. PJM McEwan, *The Dictionary of Scottish Art and Architecture*, 2004.
98. Leaflet from Mr Francis McWhirter, St. Vincent de Paul Society, Campbeltown.
99. From internet, but originally published in the Belgian nautical magazine, *Nautibel*, in 1992. Author unidentified.
100. P Moir & I Crawford, *Argyll Shipwrecks*, Wemyss Bay 1994, p 45.

101. M Steinkiste, Ostende, letter 12/10/2006.
102. *AH*, 27/5/1875.
103. RP, 844.
104. A Martin, *Fish and Fisherfolk*, *op. cit.*, pp. 24-5.
105. CC, 10/7/1948.
106. *Ibid.*, 3/11/1906.
107. *Ibid.*, 10/7/1948.
108. A Martin, *An Historical and Genealogical Tour ...* , *op. cit.*, pp. 1-2.
109. *Op. cit.* pp. 235-36.
110. Mrs F Hood, letter, 30/10/2006.
111. *AH*, 11/11/1893.
112. CC, 13/1/1919.
113. A Martin, *An Historical and Genealogical Tour ...*, *op. cit.*, p 3.
114. *Ibid.*, p 44.
115. CC, 8/3/1919.
116. *The Oxford Names Companion*, *op. cit.*, p 421; GF Black, *op. cit.* p 558.
117. CC, 11/3/1916.
118. *Ibid.*, 10/11/1932.
119. GF Black, *op. cit.*, p 550.
120. Work Horse Tax, *op. cit.*
121. CC, 3/7/1875.
122. *AH*, 18/2/1905.
123. JC Cunningham, letter 13/10/2006.
124. *AH*, 13/9/1913.
125. JC Cunningham, letter, *op. cit.*; CC, 8/5/1936, supplemented by JC Cunningham, *Alexander Campbell (1816-1905)*, a booklet compiled for private circulation in 2006.
126. JC Cunningham, booklet, *Ibid.*
127. GF Black, *op. cit.* p 811.
128. A Martin, *Kintyre: The Hidden Past*, *op. cit.*, pp. 206-7.
129. DJ McDiarmid, *100 Years of Golf at Machrihanish*, Machrihanish 1976, pp. 27-29 & 33-35; CC, 30/11/1929, and Mrs Margaret McSporran, pers. comm.

130. *CC*, 30/10/1915.
131. *Ibid*, 20/11/1915 & 8/1/1916.
132. *Who's Who in Scotland*, Irvine 2000, p 533.
133. T Mooney, *J.M. Mactavish*, Liverpool 1979.
134. CC, 20/5/1916.
135. A Martin, *Kintyre: The Hidden Past*, *op. cit.*, p 202.
136. *CC*, 1/5/1943.
137. Mr F McWhirter, pers comm, 21/10/2006.
138. *CC*, *op. cit.*
139. *The Oxford Names Companion*, *op. cit.*, p 422;   GF
      Black, *op. cit.*, p 571.
140. N Newton, 'Campbeltown at War, 1939-1945', *The
      Campbeltown Book*, Campbeltown 2003, p 352.
141. *Galloway Gazette*, 23/11/1940.
142. Surgeon's Log for HMS *Nimrod*, quoted by Stewart
      McLaughlin, e-mail 2/1/2007.
143. I Davies, letter 20/10/2006.
144. A Martin, *KM* No. 34, pp. 27-28 & No. 42, pp. 31-32; I
      Davies, *KM* No. 55, pp. 12-15 & No. 58, pp. 22-23, in all
      of which accounts primary sources are stated.
145. I Davies, 'BOAC Return Ferry Service, Summary of Aircraft
      Accidents', 2004.
146. A McKerral, *op. cit.*, p 164.
147. RP 1667, registered 25/3/1901.
148. *CC*, 26/2/1944 & 10/2/1945.
149. GF Black, *op. cit.*, p 165.
150. *John Colville, Yr., of Burnside, Campbeltown, Evangelist*,
      Edinburgh 1888, p 1.
151. D Colville, 'Notes on the Kintyre Colvilles', 1941; courtesy
      of Rory Colville.
152. *KM*, No. 9, p 3.
153. *Proceedings of the Society of Antiquaries of Scotland*, lxiv
      1929-30.
154. *KM*, *op. cit.*
155. M MacDonald, *The Campbeltown Book*, *op. cit.*, 2003,
      p 310.
156. RP, entry 987.

157. *Ibid.*, entry 381.

158. Hearth Tax List, *op. cit.*

159. *Op. cit.*

160 W Martin, 6/6/1986.

161. CC, 14/4/1894.

162. *Ibid.*, 8/4/1933.

163. W Martin, *op. cit.*

164. CC 18 & 25/5/1935.

165. Kintyre Antiquarian Library, A McEachran Collection, No. 328.

166. A Martin, *Kintyre: The Hidden Past, op. cit.*, p 112.

167. 26/11/1927.

168. Willie Mitchell, Campbeltown, quoted in *Tocher*, No. 31, p 23.

169. *Ibid.* & Rev AJ MacVicar, *The Book of Blaan, op. cit.*,   p 60.

170. J Loynachan, 'The Loynachans: Saga of a Kintyre Family', *KM* No. 66, pp. 2-6.

A Map of Kilkerran Graveyard

Notes on the Relationship Between the Text and the Map

The numbered entries in the text correspond with the numbers on the accompanying map. Both map and text utilise the divisions, or walled sections, by which the cemetery has expanded over the past 150 years. Owing to the scale of the map, absolute precision has not been possible, but by careful orientation all the enumerated gravestones should be traceable, whether or not the reader strictly follows the sequence.

A Map of KILKERRAN GRAVEYARD

indicating approximate locations
for gravestones mentioned
in this book

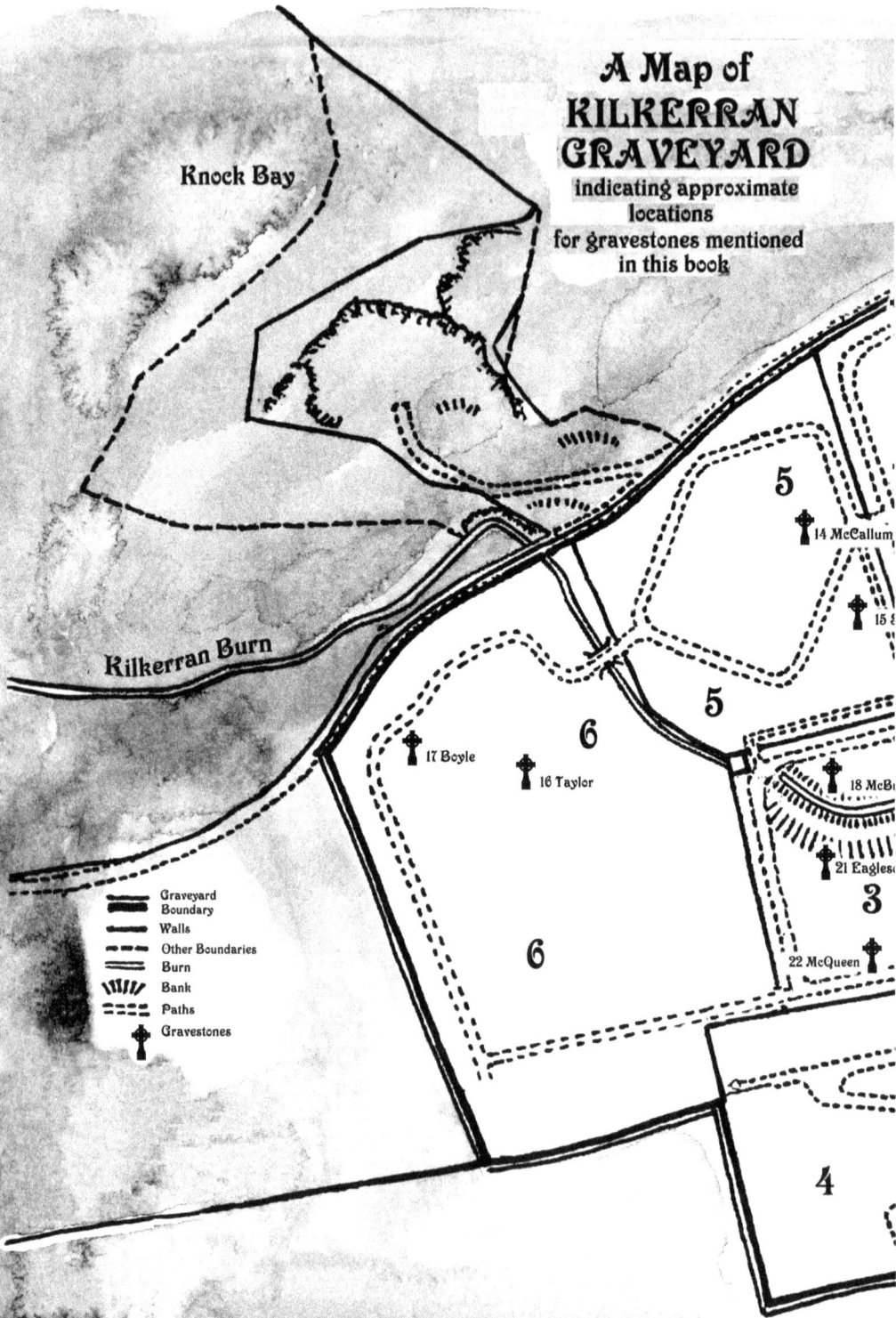

Knock Bay

Kilkerran Burn

5

14 McCallum

15 S

5

6

17 Boyle

16 Taylor

18 McB

21 Eagles

3

22 McQueen

6

4

Graveyard
Boundary

Walls

Other Boundaries

Burn

Bank

Paths

Gravestones

© George John Stewart
MMVI

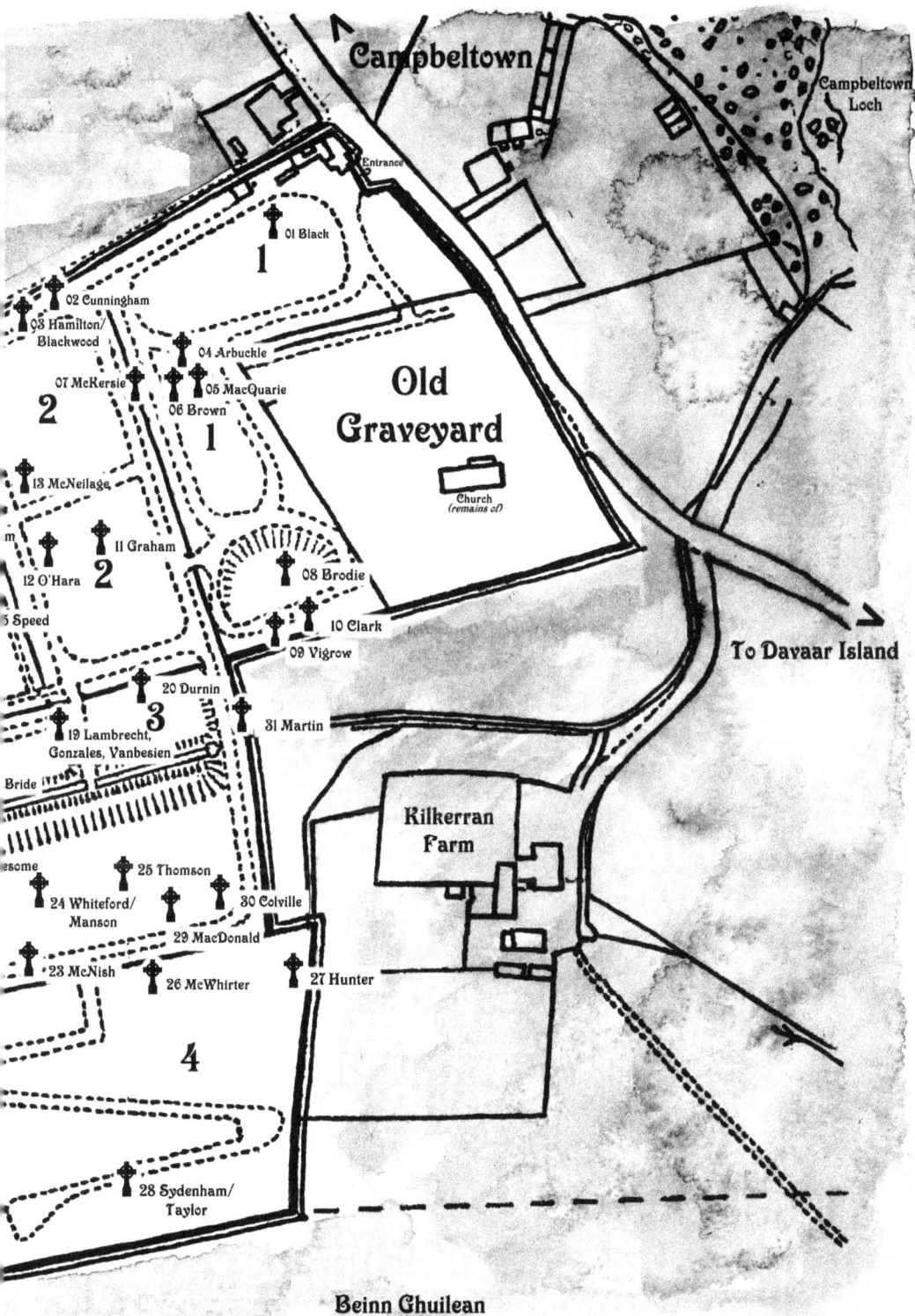

Campbeltown

Campbeltown
Loch

Entrance

01 Black

1

02 Cunningham

03 Hamilton/
Blackwood

04 Arbuckle

07 McKersie

05 MacQuarie

2

06 Brown

1

13 McNeilage

Old
Graveyard

11 Graham

2

12 O'Hara

Church
(remains of)

Speed

08 Brodie

10 Clark

09 Vigrow

To Davaar Island

20 Durnin

31 Martin

3

19 Lambrecht,
Gonzales, Vanbesien

Bride

Kilkerran
Farm

esome

25 Thomson

24 Whiteford/
Manson

30 Colville

29 MacDonald

23 McNish

26 McWhirter

27 Hunter

4

28 Sydenham/
Taylor

Beinn Ghuilean

89

Index of Family Names

In the interest of uniformity, all names which appear as *Mc-* in the main text are rendered *Mac* in this index. Original Gaelic and variant spellings of names are not listed. Likewise, individuals mentioned in the text are not indexed.

www.ingramcontent.com/pod-product-compliance
Lightning Source LLC
Chambersburg PA
CBHW060807110426
42739CB00032BA/3136